"it had to be done for Grandma and Grandpa." Mom and Dad didn't really care one way or the other.

During the time I was studying with the rabbi, his wife came into the locker next to my peephole at Eddington Pond. She was a full—blown woman, not like the school kids, and even in my innocence I knew I was seeing something special. I fell in love, at *almost* thirteen, for the second time in my life.

I continued to study with Rabbi Levine, until my bar mitzvah, and each time his wife would come into the room and talk to him, I saw her as if she was naked. It became so bad that just going to his house I got a hard—on and had to keep my books in front of me until I got into my seat. She filled my life with fantasies.

As I remember my bar mitzvah, the Torah was lifted from its sanctuary and placed flat on the raised dais and opened to the correct spot by turning both scrolls in the same direction. The Shul was half empty, unusual for a Bar mitzvah but we couldn't afford a big party so the few people we were able to invite to come to our house after services were in their seats. I handled the prayers and the reading from the Torah Scrolls very well as the old men with angelic looks in their eyes and beautiful prayer shawls pulled up over their heads as well as their shoulders, pointed to where I should begin and end. Before I could start to chant the old guys always started chanting it themselves as if I wasn't even there and I rushed to catch up. They did it with love and total devotion, although it seemed like a relay race to me. In between my parts of the service I glanced over to my right and there were the McAllisters. Mom and Dad had been discussing whether they would really show up. Boy did they look uncomfortable. I wasn't too comfortable myself.

Doing this because you really believe is one thing. Unfortunately doing it just to get it done with, is not comfort.

• • •

Cheryl Shapiro lived just down the street on Parkview, half a block below Garland facing the park. We sometimes did our homework together in high school. She had long, light brown hair, a pretty face, and a full, soft body. We got very little real schoolwork done. She tried to get me to fondle her breasts. When we kissed, she pressed herself up against me and brought my hand up to her chest, but I was afraid. I don't remember why I was afraid, only that I knew there would be consequences. I don't think I ever forgot the beating mom gave me for playing doctor in the basement of our apartment building in New York. Cheryl knew I was "safe" and just wanted to grow up with me. Only God knew how much I wanted to touch those breasts.

Cheryl was smart as a whip and really knew who she was. What attracted us to each other in the first place was our mutual distrust of religion. But she knew who she was. How did she know who she was and I still didn't seem to? Was it brains or upbringing? Did someone tell her? Cheryl felt secure in her Judaism. "It's no better, no worse than all the others," she would say.

In our tenth—grade high school social studies class, the first twenty pages of our books were stapled together. We started history with the Roman era. Cheryl took apart the pages of her book and discovered that the school had stapled together the chapter about the Hebrews. Later she showed me the pages and they contained the story of the Jews enslavement in Egypt and God sending the plagues down which forced Pharoh to free them; then Moses receiving the Ten Commandments from God.

That must have been it. The Christians followed the ten commandments too, how could they teach their children that they got them from the Jews and teach that the Jews killed Christ at the same time? Cheryl was the only one with guts enough to bring it up in class. The teacher's face was getting all red, but Cheryl wouldn't back down. "It is school policy," said the teacher, almost shouting. It was society's policy not to let the Christian children know where they came from. Unfortunately, I didn't know where I came from, either.

4

Knee Surgery, Mom's Death,
and Life in the Navy
1944–1948

My first and only dance at the Garland Street junior high school was a bust. We did a kind of hoedown, changing partners and touching hands, and as we did so, the girls would pull down their sleeves so my hand wouldn't touch theirs. I didn't realize what was going on at first, but when I did I became mortified and immediately left the dance. The long walk home in the cold didn't bother me. My face was flushed and red, burning with this latest insult. I never went to another of the dances there. I should have realized something like that would happen. Just the previous week I met two of my classmates in town. Gloria Owen and Sue Klein were window shopping, and I saw them in the window bay of Viner's shoe store and said hello. Gloria turned and said hello and we talked a bit, but Sue wouldn't turn toward me. "Sue, its Murry," said Gloria, showing a little discomfort. No response. Gloria leaned toward Sue and whispered, "What's wrong with you, it's Murry Handler."

"He's a Jew," was all Sue would answer, another hard slap in the face for me.

"Sue," I said, "your father is a Jew."

"But I'm not," she answered and hurried down the street with Gloria in tow, looking back at me, apologizing with a gesture of her free hand.

• • •

The captains of the football teams were picked by Coach Raymond. Then the captains chose from the guys who showed up and wanted to be on the team. There were only two Jews that year, Mel Wagner and me, and we were not picked until everyone was chosen for each team. We were the only two left and each captain, even though one was Jerry McAlister who lived downstairs in the same house, chose me with great reluctance. My understanding of the reasons for this, are different now. Jerry couldn't let his Christian friends think he liked a Jew, so he did what peer pressure demanded.

I spent the entire year practicing, but never once in that entire year was I thrown the ball. I played left end and felt I should have been involved in at least some passes. On the last game of the year I was tired of going through the motions. Jerry threw me a pass that would have tied up our score with the opposing team. I wasn't ready for or expecting it, and the ball flew right through my hands when I leapt for it at the last moment. Shit, things would be much worse for the Jewish kids going out for the team next year.

Both my knees went bad before I got out of junior high. In Maine, junior high football was a six-man team with a smaller ball. Because of the fewer players there was more open field hitting, and that's how I got it. It wasn't any one time getting blocked or tackling someone and everyone piling on top. It was an accumulation of hits that finally ripped my cartiledge in a place I didn't expect.

I was at the Dow Air Force Base playing Basketball with the airmen. Two of my Jr. High School classmates; Pete Alow, Ed Sleigh and I walked about four miles from the house to get into a pick—up game there. I leaped to make a shot and when I came down my right leg crumbled under me. I tried several times to stand but couldn't. The leg was painful and useless. None of us had a nickel to call our families and we didn't dare call home for help at this late hour anyway. Pete and Ed literally dragged and carried me, stopping and starting again all the way home. They left me at the doorstep. They were Christians and wouldn't come inside.

At first I was proud of the injuries—it gave me a certain macho standing. The pain, the hard road back, and a number of other incidents sobered me up.

At fourteen, waking up after my first knee operation, I saw Mom sitting besides my bed crying. The last time I remembered her crying was when they had to sell her engagement ring, so even as I awoke from the anesthesia I was concerned that things were worse than they should be. A few hours later I was the one doing the crying. My leg was in a cast up to my hip, and the pain was excruciating. I screamed for them to remove the cast and must have impressed them enough so that Doc Rhulin, a great guy, who looked more like an ex fighter than a surgeon, came to my room. This wasn't Bangor General, the big hospital. This was a regular house with a porch around the front and no more than ten beds in the whole place. I was in a large room that looked like a front parlor with a fireplace,

66

polished hardwood floors, and shiny white walls with lace curtains letting light filter in softly. There were other beds in the room but none of them was occupied.

Doc Rhulin cut the cast open and my leg swelled up faster than my grandma's bread dough that rose in the enameled pan next to the stove. It looked like a pink watermelon with a giant scar. Two nurses, one on each side, held me down by my arms while Rhulin squeezed together a pair of metal tongs, inserted them into my incision, and then released them. Liquid poured out of the wound. I threw both nurses backward against the wall, sat bolt upright, and shouted, "Holy shit." The nurses were on me again in seconds. The doc dug around a while in my knee, releasing all kinds of gunk that slid around the sides of that huge melon and down onto my bed. Sweet relief.

One of the nurses who I threw against the wall must have seen something she liked. She started coming into my room late at night and shaving her legs with her foot up against my bed. I saw what I thought she was offering, but she was strictly there for show. Two years later, at age sixteen, Doc Rhulin performed the same operation on my other knee. Three months after that, I enlisted in the navy.

• • •

My Uncle Lou owned a summer place at Chemo Pond, which Mainers called a camp. It was right at the water, on a bank about fifteen feet above the pond, with steep, dark green stairs and railing that led down along the bare earth of the bank to the dock. The silver, weathered dock with its tire halves nailed to the sides jutted out twenty feet or so into deep water. In the summer when the lilies were in bloom they seemed to band the pond about thirty feet from the shore. As the sun went down we would fish for white perch, trolling back and forth up the center of the pond. A bushel basket full of fish was not out of the ordinary. The call of the loon was the last thing I remember at night, as sleep took me.

Memories of my mother relaxing there are some of the best I still have of her. That's also where I first became aware of her illness and watched her puke up green stuff. I listened to the furtive whispering of Dad and Uncle Lou about buying some dope down on Hancock St. to dull her pain. I wish they had explained things to me. Mom was a good person, a hard working woman and a wonderful mother. Where was the justice in this? Where was God?

After an operation to remove some of the cancerous growth from her stomach, the Doctor told Dad, "they were as big as grapefruit." We had Mom for about another year and a half. We went everywhere together in what seemed to be a rush all the time. Sure, she knew there was very little time left. I knew too but wouldn't face up to it. When she didn't feel well, I wouldn't let her sit or rest—I couldn't. I was afraid that if she stopped doing things she would die.

Mom was laid out in the front room on top of a table, in an unfinished pine hexagonal box that made her seem very small. This was the way religious Jews buried their dead. We know Dad wasn't particularly religious, but this was also cheap. Family and friends came in to view her and pay their respects. They walked along one side of the coffin, around the front end, and then back out of the room, tisking all the way. I couldn't accept the permanence and irreversibility of death. I fully expected Mom to stop lying there and get up and make us dinner.

Every now and then I still wake up in a cold sweat, feeling my head being pulled down into Mom's coffin, right over her face, by a man on the other side. Pulling my tie with his left hand, his other hand was slicing my suit lapels with a razor blade. Old religious Jews did things like that. This guy wanted me to be a part of what he considered was necessary for the occasion. Dad grabbed the man and pushed him back, yelling at him in what little Yiddish he knew. That was one of the few times I saw my father take strong action that wasn't directed at me or someone else in the family. This outburst from my father had the same effect on him as hitting the drunk in front of our apartment building in New York, the one who was bothering Mom. Dad staggered as if *he* had been pushed hard.

The street below, which I could see from our second—story window, had about fifty Jews milling around, some coming up the front stairs taking their turns viewing my mom. Looking down on them from above, the yarmulkes looked like a sea of black and white dots, moving to prearranged positions so a line could be drawn that connected them all and might help make some sense out of this enormous happening.

In a neighborhood that found it difficult putting up with just one Jewish family, this outpouring must have been very strange for them. There was no name calling this time, no problems—the occasion was too solemn. It was June 1944, and there was another solemn occasion on a massive scale happening far away from us as we were saying good—bye to Mom. The invasion of Normandy was taking place, and there would be grieving around the country as news of the dead came in.

My grief at Mom's death was experienced alone and at night. We never grieved as a family. If it were Dad who died and not Mom, she would have shown us how. She understood things. She talked to us. At seventy, I still grieve alone for my mother. It has become a habit. Hard as I try—and I do often—I can't remember Mom's actual burial, not even a part of it. I guess I shoved that pain so far back in my psyche that it can never be reached.

At the time, fear overpowered grief. I was sixteen years old, immature, and petrified of death. I just wanted it over with.

Truly facing death as an adult came late in life for me when my wife and I moved to North Carolina in 1992. Our neighbors there, Don and Gloria Halisey, became friends. I really enjoyed sitting at the edge of our pool, dangling my feet in the water, sipping a cocktail, and talking with Don. His love was airplanes. He could talk about the subject all day. He must have been important to the airlines as a trouble—shooter, because they wouldn't let him retire. He kept going back for more when they called. He finally did retire, and not long after that was diagnosed with cancer. I felt a great need to see him frequently at the hospital and visit with him during his last days at home. There was a bond between us. Don felt that my experience with my son Evan and his miraculous survival from cancer might have given me answers that could help him. I think Don also knew I needed to do this. To finally face, without fear, someone dying and understand that it was going to happen. He helped me more than I realized at that time. I want to believe that he was aware of helping me and that I helped him some, too.

• • •

Toward the end of my high school career, Dad was impossible to live with and seemed as eager to get one hungry mouth out of the house as I was to be out from under what I felt was his tyranny. His expectations of what I must do were overwhelming. Cook, clean and look after Bob as well as keep up with school. I wanted to have some fun. I wanted to run away from death. From the moment he came home from work he was out of control with grief for Mom and his expectations of me.

There was no way for me to get an education beyond high school. Dad wouldn't pay one cent for it, and my grades were not good enough for scholarships. Actually my grades were in the cellar. This last couple of years with Mom dying, schoolwork didn't seem important at all. Dad's words of encouragement were, "You haven't got the head for college. I won't waste my money. Go to a trade school and learn a trade." The way my grades had deteriorated, he was right, but I already had four more years of schooling than he did and I felt that his suggestion had something to do with this. I had remained in the pre—college courses and felt a trade school was beneath me even though I was obviously very talented in drawing and painting. Art school was an ambition of mine but trade schools were looked down on by my group of Jewish friends, who would go on to become accountants, doctors, and lawyers or go into their fathers' businesses. I did not want to be a junk man. That meant living poor and doing dirty work and smelling of rusted metal all the time, just like Dad.

On some Saturdays, (the Jewish Sabbath) my dad took me with him to help with the work. One particular Saturday we went to a private farmhouse Dad had made arrangements with earlier. It was tiny for a farmhouse, more like a big shack. It looked like a toy that someone had placed smack dab in the middle of a dirt field with no connection to the land around it; a surreal, almost Dali—like painting and I was just another prop.

It had probably been a working farm many years ago, but it was sadly neglected now. There were no foundation shrubs or trees to protect the house from the wind and very little insulation in the walls. The doors didn't close properly, and you could see newspapers stuffed around the door jams and window frames.

The homeowner was burning old shoes in the wood stove in the basement, because they gave off a lot of heat and were free. Most of the shoes had metal taps on them, and that's what we were after. My guess was that this man worked at Viner's Shoe Factory, a locally famous leather goods name, and brought discarded used shoes home from work to burn.

Dad knew Viner. Dad took a AAA shoe width and a size ten shoe, and so did Mr. Viner himself, so Dad broke in his shoes for him. Back then, leather shoes were stiff as boards when you bought them. Mr. Viner as the owner of a leather factory and a shoe store didn't have to bust his feet breaking in new shoes. Dad got to wear new shoes several times a year for about three weeks each time. I always thought it was a strange way to do things.

In the basement of the ramshackle house we sifted through clouds of fine silt so thick I could barely see my father in front of me. My coughing from the silt became extreme, and I began to gag. I couldn't vomit—the dry dust wouldn't allow it, I couldn't swallow. I panicked and ran up the storm cellar stairs and took a cloud of silt with me that seemed to encircle my body even in the open air. I dry—heaved on my hands and knees while

Dad continued sifting for the metal taps. I felt guilty and ashamed, but I refused to go back into the cellar when Dad called to me. He was pissed, but didn't force me. When we got home he let Mom know that I wasn't good for much. There were other times that were better between us. I promised myself that I would not spend my life like that.

Dad and Grandpa jointly bought the Brewer scrap drive. During World War II, towns held scrap drives to collect any metal that was lying around and not being used. This was a big scrap drive, and the town of Brewer used an empty lot that was just over the Bangor—Brewer bridge and up the hill I hitchhiked from.

On the trucks we piled junk and scrap and old file cabinets, clothes hangers, pots and pans, spikes, toys, motors, car parts, and a large door from a bank vault. Dad, Mom, Willy the hired man and I, all tried to lift that vault door. We got one end of the bank vault door onto the back of the old Model T, but we couldn't budge it from there. My grandfather was watching us from where he was loading his truck. He came over, waved us aside, knelt down, and with one hand shoved that door up onto the truck with such force that the truck shuddered under a cloud of dust and looked like it would collapse. Grandpa's work habits were the same as his eating habits—he did it alone. We all stood there with our mouths open while Grandpa went back to work. With that kind of strength my grandpa could fight anybody, I thought—and win too. But he never fought. He took insults and name calling and kept going.

He never forgot the time the police put him in jail for slapping a man. He almost decapitated him. The man came up in front of Grandpa, opened a hand full of ground pepper, and threw it in his face yelling, "Jew bastard." Temporarily blinded, Grandpa swung out blindly to protect himself and backhanded the man across the side of his head. The man was in the hospital for weeks. When the sheriff found out what happened from neighbors who had witnessed the confrontation, Grandpa was let out of jail. He was only in there two nights, but he never forgot it and neither did the town. Nobody bothered him much after that.

Dad and Grandpa, with no love lost between them before this, disputed the money from the scrap drive, thinking each had cheated the other and another nail was driven into the fence between the families.

•   •   •

There were three other Bangor high school students who went with me to enlist in the navy. All had top marks in school and were already enrolled in college. Not one of them passed the physical. Zip was too fat. Goody, our school's best trumpet player, walked in his sleep. Pamer, the brain, was blind without his glasses and I could barely walk because of my recent knee surgery.

I couldn't do any of the deep knee bends required in the physical exam. The navy induction doctor took me aside and asked why I was eager to get in with such bad legs. I told him that "Doc Rhulin had just removed a torn cartilage from my right knee. The left one was working okay though." I explained about not being able to pay for college and two years in the navy would get me four years in school on the GI Bill. He was a nice guy and must have sensed the desperation in my voice. He signed my card and passed me on with a pat on the shoulder. I don't even remember his name or what he looked like. The only sports cripple of the bunch and I made it in. Don't get me wrong, I was not much of an athlete, just stubborn and determined to play a game I was eminently unsuited for.

"As an enlisted man you can choose any place in the world to serve," I was told. And I believed the recruiting officer who said that, so I chose Atlantic sea duty. See the world and all that stuff. You guessed it. I got Pacific land duty. Really. Twenty one months in Hawaii, after the mandatory boot camp training in Baimbridge, Maryland. Maryland was a place that turned out to be more dangerous to American servicemen than combat itself. I was out of my league there. Gang guys from the streets of New York, corn huskers from Minnesota, paper mill workers from Massachusetts, French Canadian loggers from Maine, and me, a Jew. I refer to myself not as *from* somewhere, as I did the others, but just as the Jew. That's because it didn't make any difference where I was from. To them I was the Jew, period. Fortunately for me, one of the toughest gang guys from Brooklyn was also a Jew and I would enlist his help from time to time. Once the others knew I was "connected" they left me pretty much alone.

Black servicemen were segregated to their own barracks and ate at separate sections in the mess hall. The hate espoused for the black servicemen, the fear, was not new to me—it was just pointed in a different direction. The scuttlebutt of rioting blacks, the knives we white guys stuck into our bedposts for quick access, it was all bullshit. It was all made up to conceal fear and ignorance and maybe, just maybe, that was the same interaction going on between them and me.

Since I was the only one of the recruits with three years of high school ROTC (I didn't tell them it was in the band

75

playing a clarinet), the chief petty officer grudgingly gave me the job of guide—on. Instead of carrying a heavy rifle, I carried a wooden dowel with the company flag and marched out front as a guide for the troop to follow. A plush job to be sure, but I was on my toes every second. The petty officer was waiting to put his imprint on me as he did to many of the others—his foot up their ass when they miss stepped or lagged, and I mean UP. "C'mon y'all stoopid sonsabitches, how fuckin' stoopid are you Yankees? Hey there, you pelican muthah fuckah, get your ass up to the line. The next time you misstep, asshole, I'll be up yours so far you'll thaank you have a second tongue."

I learned words and phrases from my superior officer that certainly weren't in the manual, but I picked some up and thought it was cool. Although I was afraid of him all the time, his ability to spew out a constant stream of invectives without taking a breath seemed admirable to me at seventeen.

About three weeks into boot camp I bumped into Herb, a guy from Bangor who was always bullying everybody when we were in High School. Remember Gloria who I met when she was shopping with Sue Klein, who didn't want to be a Jew? Gloria was Herb's girl. Herb was one of the town toughs. I remember wrestling a ball away from him on the basketball court once, and he was furious—ashamed actually. His manhood was being challenged. I think if Coach Raymond hadn't been there he would have hit me, he was that mad. He came up to me after the game and asked if I wanted to fight. *Here we go again,* I thought. Without hesitation I said, "No," and took a step back just to be sure this wasn't a repeat performance. My poor jaw couldn't take another punch. Later, one of my Jewish friends who overheard the exchange admonished me for not fighting him. "We can't let them feel that we are afraid," he said to me.

Herb was so glad to see someone from home and so frightened of his first few days in camp that he treated me like a long—lost friend. About a week later, Herb contracted cat fever, an imitation of malaria. A good imitation—I had been there already so I knew about it, but it was not a recurring disease, as malaria is. Herb was like a baby. I visited him in his barracks every day until I shipped out, and I wondered why we were all afraid of him back in Bangor.

Just after boot camp when I was on leave in New York, my dad got married again. His timing was perfect, and I was able to attend as one of the four people who held up the chuppah. A chuppah is a cloth covering representing the temple that Jews have their wedding ceremony under when it's not in a temple. Dad was fifty years old, and Sadye said she was forty—eight. (We found out years later, when one of her sisters made a cake for a surprise birthday party and it said seventy-five, that she had been sixty—one at the wedding, making her older than Dad.

The night of their wedding we all stayed at Dr. Mailman's house. Dr. Sam Mailman was a down—to—earth straight shooter. A clean—shaven Russian peasant who had struck it rich in America. He had a huge stomach like my grandfather, except his was soft and mushy and he wore clean, starched shirts with cufflinks. Sam was married to Sadye's sister Lee and lived in the faded grandness of a wonderful old Brooklyn mansion where he kept his offices as well. The ceilings were high and made up of small, square, raised walnut wood panels with a light bulb socket in the center of each one. The staircase coming down from the second floor was six feet wide with a grand walnut railing and curved bottom two steps. The foyer was as generous as Grandma's was tiny. No light bulbs hanging on a cord here.

When my dad emerged the next morning, I was sitting with Sam, having breakfast. Sam called to Dad as he saw him coming down the stairs. "Well, how was it Ben?"

My dad, not realizing that his new wife was behind him, called back and said, "It fits."

Sadye's gasp was the first inkling Dad or Sam had that she was on the upper part of the staircase. She turned and went back upstairs to the bedroom and didn't come down again until dinner. The two men just laughed. They were convulsed, mildly embarrassed, and thought it was funny as hell. At eighteen I seemed to be more embarrassed for them than they were. It may have been funny for a man, but not with the bride right there. I thought it was cruel as hell.

• • •

I made several close friends while in the navy—Russ Lahoy from Lowell, Massachusetts; Dick Ruel from Maine; Bill Ames from Missouri; and Maximino Asuelo Kinsey from the Philippines. I lost touch with Ruel after boot camp, but the rest stayed with me in Hawaii, at a small base called Lualualei on the west side of Oahu.

The trip overseas on a Liberty ship is still painful to recall. Our quarters were below decks in small, airless rooms. Sleeping was in a five—tier set—up of bunks, one over the other. Mine was the top bunk with a steam pipe running over my stomach, one foot away. Turning over became a major maneuver. What I didn't realize was that the top bunk listed far more than the bottom bunk when the ship hit rough weather, and I had to literally hang on to the sides or fall out onto the deck.

I got seasick the first night out and stayed that way for the next five days. I wasn't alone by any means. Picture this: the mess hall was a stand-up affair. Five sailors behind a counter, each one serving something different but indistinguishable, slapped it on your metal tray as you passed by. Then you juggled it to the stand-up counters to eat as the ship lurched and was pounded by the waves.

Food and vomit flew in all directions, and few of us could withstand this onslaught. The cook's sense of humor was obvious—serve a bunch of new recruits those semi—green hot dogs on their first night out in a storm, and if they live . . . well that's the rub, most of us didn't want to live. I found a place up on deck in the surround of an open—topped 20mm gun emplacement and in the storm and rain stayed there for five days and nights, vomiting and praying for death to take me.

The head (bathroom), was something only the hardiest of us ventured into. Metal troughs ran the length of both sides of a long, narrow room. Water flowed constantly in one direction in these open troughs, washing the excrement away, except when the ship hit bad weather. Then the waste was sloshed back upstream, and you had better have a cast—iron stomach.

We docked and disembarked at Pearl Harbor, and I wondered how anyone could fight a war under these conditions. What a dirty, ragtag, smelly bunch of kids. We were put on assigned buses each with its own destinations.

Our driver was a clean, spiffy, navy old-timer wearing a sharply pressed uniform with his hat set squarely on his head. As we stopped at different bases, he called out the names of the recruits who were to get off. Several hours later, after traveling past much island scrub and letting almost everyone else off, the bus reached Lualualei Naval Base. My name and Russ Lahoy's was called, and we got off. After looking at our papers the marine guard at the gate told us to report to the galley to Chief Petty Officer Raskin.

Chief Raskin was about thirty years old, slightly stooped with a pencil mustache and sweat breaking through his shirt under his arms and around his neck. He wore open-collared chief's grays, a clean white T shirt with a sweat stained, black visored cap, and carried what seemed to be a list with our names. "Which one of you wants to be the base butcher? We need a butcher for the fourteenth naval district. Haven't had one for almost a year now," the chief said. Russ and I looked at each other. I thought, *who the hell wants to be a butcher?* I didn't sign up for that. *It's bad enough they screwed me out of getting Atlantic sea duty,* I thought.

"Okay, we'll flip a coin," said the chief. "Call it, Handler," he said as he tossed a quarter in the air.

I called heads, it came up tails. I became the new butcher for the navy's fourteenth naval district, which encompassed all of Hawai'i and ships at sea. Walter Winchel with a meat cleaver. Russ wound up cutting grass for eighteen months and was very happy doing just that.

Chief Raskin took me on a tour of my new empire, shook my hand, welcomed me aboard, and then turned me over to the head cook, a dirty, fat, old navy salt who wasn't anyone Mom would say to bring home to dinner. Downwind in a storm you would know where he was. He gave me the week's menu, helped me carry in a hindquarter of frozen beef from one of the outside reefers, and hung it on the hook dangling from crossed metal angle irons just below the ceiling. He shook my hand and welcomed me aboard, too. I couldn't wait to wash.

At three the next morning, as ordered, I stumbled into my cutting room with the beef—cutting book under my arm and turned on the lights. Everything was moving. The beef skin seemed to be turning round its own leg, the floors were sliding into the blood drain, the wall paint was disappearing into cracks. For a few moments, I couldn't pull it together. But when the floor was suddenly crawling up my pant legs, I knew what it was—roaches. Three—inch—long tropical roaches with wings, a single, unbroken mass of them. I learned slowly, through trial and error, to tie my pants legs before turning on the light, to step back until all the roaches disappeared, and to always, *always* leave them an escape route. I also became quite a fair butcher and took pride in my ability to cut a great roast.

A reefer is a humongous, stainless—steel, walk—in refrigerator, and I had four of them: three for storing vegetables and one for keeping frozen meat, plus a ten—by—ten—foot cutting room with knives, apron, sharpening stones, and a floor drain for the blood. Several times during my butcher days I would cut or stab myself and run through the mess hall with everyone sitting and eating to get across to the medic on the other side of the building. One day I walked into the only reefer without a lever to open the door from the inside, and it locked behind me. I panicked and started pounding on the door and yelling. Fortunately for me, Bill Ames had just come out back looking for me and heard the noise. Normally, no one but me was out there. For a few moments I thought it would be my own private veggy morgue.

Bill was a wonderful guy—a tall, easygoing Missourian who could get along with anyone. We had a lot in common. Our dads hadn't talked to or spent much time with us and we both seemed to be still suffering from that neglect. He joined the navy for the same reasons I did—to get away from home and to get the GI Bill benefits.

The nineteen months I spent in Hawaii was not a deliberate planning time for my future. Maturity, personal growth, and an understanding of what I might do with my life, did begin to come into focus though.

The base commander helped with part of my education by bringing in busloads of local girls for the personnel. He kept a few for himself until his wife arrived unannounced from the States and ended his philandering. The officers were grateful to me for painting murals of game birds in wall panels around their club, so I was able to drink there at will. I had always been a natural in drawing and painting in school and really enjoyed it. A career in art seemed imminent.

High-ranking naval officers from around the Pacific came into my butcher shop, put their arm around my shoulder, and made illegal requests for special cuts of beef and got them at my chiefs insistence. I reminded him of his own permissiveness when he threatened me over a missing canned ham during an inventory. Several seamen had come to me and requested a main course at a birthday party. That was where the canned ham went, and they certainly deserved it as much as the brass did. I learned about women, crotch crabs, gambling, and even more foul language. I also learned that most of these men were just like me—waiting to get out.

After six months I was tired of hauling and cutting sides of beef, dodging flying roaches, and driving a twenty—ton trailer to Pearl Harbor every other week for supplies. One of these trips almost killed me. I had asked for Russ Lahoy to assist me so we could spend some time together. The lawns kept him outside and we couldn't talk to each other for days on end. On the way back from Pearl, on a curve just past a tiny bridge, the entire back of the truck turned over. At first I only realized that the front wheel on my side was off the ground. Imagine trying to quickly judge what was able to lift up a fully loaded twenty tonner. Russ was sitting to my right in the cab and as my side went up, his went down. In a flash he clawed his way over me, the wheel, and with his feet on my head, face, and shoulders pushed himself out my door, which was by this time pointing straight up in the air. I crawled out after him, astonished at what he had just accomplished.

Vegetables and beef were strewn over what seemed like acres of road and fields. The truck body had ripped off one side of the frame and pulled the cab over after it. We checked each other out; except for minor bruises on me, which I got from his boots, we seemed to be okay. Russ walked to the nearest phone to report the accident, but it took hours for someone from the base to show up. We had plenty of raw cabbage and fruits to eat while waiting, but the frozen meat was rotting in front of us. We couldn't do a thing except direct other cars and trucks around us and the produce.

The navy held a preliminary inquiry and Chief Raskin, somewhat gleefully, told me I was looking at a court—martial inquiry. The truck was examined, and they found that the maintenance crew had neglected to replace the bolts on the right side where the body attaches to the frame. Relieved and angry at being presumed guilty of reckless driving, I requested an immediate transfer to become a radio operator. I didn't know a thing about it, but it had to be a cleaner place to work in and maybe had some nicer people, too.

• • •

Wild dogs that roamed the island sometimes got on the base and in their confusion couldn't find their way out. These were large and dangerous animals. Most of them looked like gaunt German Police dogs who had been turned loose years ago or escaped from their pens. When we headed for the beach about two miles away, we always went as a group. A pack of these dogs would follow us at a respectable distance and disappear as we got to the beach or back to the base. They never attacked us. I wondered if they yearned for human companionship or thought we had some food.

One time I heard a commotion in back of the barracks and saw a frightened wild dog trying desperately to get away and at the same time hide itself behind some garbage pails that banged around and added to the poor animals confusion. Whenever someone tried to get near, it snarled and snapped viciously. One of the guys went for a pistol and the boatswains mate pumped three 45s into the poor animal before it went down in a bloody mess, yelping with fright.

Lualualei had the largest radio transmitting building in the Pacific. I was assigned to it, given a book, and told to study. Sound familiar? The building was huge and built in the form of a cross (just what I needed). My new boss, Jim, was another Southern boy—a real gentleman and a pleasure to work for. Jim was from North Carolina, and I believe he had spent some time in college or might even have had his degree from the University of North Carolina. He was just what a Northerner would expect a Southern gentleman to look like: tall, slight of build, sensitive face, and a grace of movement that shouted "Ashley."

The radio frequency was brutal, and no effort was made to protect us. I could hold a fluorescent tube with one hand on each end and it would blink off and on with any of the code passing through at the time. This meant it was passing through my body as well. I couldn't do this for long without burning my hands. I wondered what it would do to the family jewels. The combination of this radio frequency and the x—rays of my scalp as a kid when I had ringworm did worry me some.

Tuning the transmitters to connect with specific ships in the Pacific fleet was our prime mission. Radio frequency coming through the dials burned tiny white pin dots in our fingertips and kept them in a constant state of pain and sensitivity. This sensitivity helped us tune in the fleet more accurately than we would otherwise be able to.

The most difficult thing for me at age eighteen in my new job was staying awake. We were short of manpower, and my shift was twenty—four hours on, twenty-four hours off. I would fall asleep standing up, leaning against a wall, almost anywhere. I would sit at the central console area in front of the tuners and fall asleep with my eyes open. I would be cleaning out the connection points inside one of the transmitters, a dangerous job, and would fall totally asleep. Two men were electrocuted during my eighteen months at the base doing the same work.

The console area was a complete circle at the confluence of all four branches of the cross that made up the shape of the building. There were fifty two transmitters in this one building,

85

most of them so big you could walk into them. One night the commander made a surprise inspection, and I never saw him. I was asleep, sitting in the console in front of a tuner, with my eyes open. After this I vowed to overcome my inability to stay awake. I was putting the entire watch in jeopardy. It was extremely difficult, but in about a month, with Jim's help, I succeeded by not sitting down. I would literally fall to my knees, asleep. The pain in my knees became more important than the sleep.

My first night of serious poker playing in the boiler room of the transmitter building became a maneuver for position in the hierarchy of seamen on the base. I was a somewhat gullible kid and wanted to please. So when Dan, a snotty guy who would like to have been a real bully but didn't have the nerve, asked me to take my turn and inspect the perimeter of the building, I agreed. I had no idea that they would be waiting at one of the corners, in the dark, trying to scare the hell out of me. The perimeter was erratic and vast, with scrub growth and animal noises all around. What they didn't know was my background—I may be scared to death, but only my insides show it.

I never even twitched when they jumped out of the dark and screamed. I turned and quietly asked what they were doing there. It destroyed them. "You knew, you son of a bitch, you knew," Dan yelled at me.

"How could I know?" I asked. "No one said a word to me. I don't scare like that." My position in the hierarchy moved up.

Our base set up a five—man basketball team with Jim as captain, and I got on it, bad legs and all. I still couldn't bend the left one very well, but running and jumping didn't seem to bother me. I was young.

I went into Pearl Harbor on a pass only once in my eighteen months on Oahu. A group of us went: a guy named Waller, whom everyone teased because he acted effeminate, so they called him a fag; Mike, a tough navy regular; and a guy named Bush, a big handsome young man who would just as soon kill you as talk to you. They pressed Waller to get his picture taken with a native gal who would give you a quick rub-off at the same time. Waller protested, but he eventually went into the booth to prove his manhood and came out with his badge of courage, a wet spot on the front of his pants. They still called him a fag.

Honolulu was not a pretty place at the end of the war, and the Hawaiians wanted the servicemen gone. We had used up their island and their women, and I could feel their animosity. Who needed this? I could understand it, but who needed it. I never went back to town.

Bush and I were fooling around in the barracks one evening and he was smoking a cigar. Before I knew it, I was on my back, on the floor, with Bush on me burning a hole in my right wrist with the cigar. His buddy, whom everyone called Tex started shouting, "Burn the fuckin' Jew, burn him." At first I couldn't believe what was happening. *Where did this suddenly come from? Does it just lie dormant in every Christian's heart,* I wondered? *When will they have enough?* I pulled myself free and rolled over into a kneeling position, but before I could get up Tex had his huge hand on back of my neck and I was pinned to the ground again. This time he kept me there, laughing and cursing me. I couldn't move. This was a lot more difficult than getting the drooling old lady off me. There was a former divinity student who knew me, and he was just standing there. I

87

implored him to intervene. "Why should I help you? I know why you're asking me, and that's no reason for me to help you—shit."

Hate, it seems, is like a bad cold. People see it and catch it. We dropped an atomic bomb on Hiroshima this day, and these assholes found more interest in degrading a Jew than understanding the scorched humanity and the implications of an atomic era. It took a couple of weeks for the blister on my wrist to heal, and I didn't fool around with Bush any more.

Here's another Bush story. Our base barber was a Japanese woman; her family lived in Honolulu. I was on my way to get a haircut and was stopped by one of Bush's buddies.

"You can't get a haircut now, Murry."

"Why not?" I asked.

With a shitty grin he told me that other friends were guarding the other side of the building because Bush was in fucking the barber. I couldn't believe what he was telling me. I knew that Bush thought all the women wanted him and were just too shy to ask, so he forced on them what they were too shy to ask for. I didn't think he would pull something like that on the base though.

I went for my haircut the next day and the barber looked terrible. I wanted to shout at her "Why did you let him do it?" and then I remembered my burned wrist and I knew. Word got around the base, and the barber who had been forced into sex was fired. What could a Japanese woman, although she was an American citizen, do about anything while we were fighting Japan?

• • •

During the time I was stationed at Lualualei in Hawaii, one of my interests was diving for shells and I had accumulated a considerable amount of semiprecious stones, which I sent home for Dad to keep until I got out of the military.

The first thing out of his mouth, when he answered my knock on the door wasn't hello or a hug after almost two years away but a tirade about the bag I had sent home. Dad hadn't changed much. He was the same as when I left, fearful of everything around him with a special fear of being dirt poor again. When I deciphered what he was telling me, I realized that he didn't have the bag any more. "Dad, what happened to the shells? I dived for two years to collect those shells. There were cat's eyes and ambers in there." I was trying to impress on him that it was worth money. He simply said that he threw the bag out. The shells went the way of my rifle, my saxophone and clarinet. He sold those for money, but the shells didn't bring him any cash.

Years later my wife, Enid, on hearing this story, came up with the answer. The bag of shells, which was large and heavy, must have required more postage when it arrived and he wouldn't pay it. If he had known what those cat's eyes were selling for, he would have. Nothing had changed; certainly Dad was as difficult as ever, even with his new wife, Sadye.

• • •

I teased others in the Navy without realizing I was doing it. Ralph, one of the really nice guys on the base requested a transfer. He was a pudgy, stoop—shouldered guy with a big mustache and spoke with a genuine twang and could easily have been a saloon character in a western movie. He was as nice a guy as could be and wouldn't hurt a fly. When I heard the news of his transfer request, I went to him and asked if it was because of me, and he reluctantly said that it was. I had transferred the shit I took all the time to Ralph by teasing him about his weight and his funny way of speaking. The enormity of what I had done struck me with such force that as I asked him if I was at fault I stood in front of him with tears in my eyes. "Please don't leave," I implored him. "I didn't realize that it was so bad, I promise I will stop it."

Ralph was gone within the week. My shame was overwhelming. I had done to him what was done to me. I transferred the hate, my insecurity, Mom's death, Dad's neglect, the Rolsky family rejection, everything that was rotting in me, to him. Today, when I think of Ralph, shame still washes over me.

5

Back to the Real World

We boarded the plane in Pearl Harbor early one morning in January of 1948. Because the navy kept a group of us in Hawai'i past our enlisted time, our commander got us a berth going home on the flying boat *Mars*. The *Mars* was a two—storied monster seaplane made of plywood, with four huge props attached to one giant wing overhead. What a difference this would be from the way we came over on that Liberty ship! Russ Lahoy was on board and promised to come with me to visit my Aunt Esta, who had a new husband and lived in Forest Hills, New York. I had communicated with her during my navy time, and she was going to give me a place to stay while I looked for work and tried to get into art school. All through grade and high school I was always drawing, doing the class posters and portraits of fellow students. Even with the G I Bill in hand, it seems I would still go to a trade school as my father said I should.

The plane was jammed with sailors and marines. Many women and children, the families of officers, were also on board. The inside of the plane was unfinished with construction struts showing. The seating area was minimal—most of us found our own niche on top of duffel bags or in little nooks and crannies between the ribs of the plane. The one bathroom on each level was primitive by any standard. The men could stand and pee into a small dark hole raised about a foot off the floor. The women had a special tube with a crescent-shaped contraption on the end so they could stand and pee. Sitting down was dangerous, and no one did. I guess that's why they didn't feed us on the trip back.

To pull this huge hull out of the water meant breaking a bond between the plane and the surface tension. The take-off took at least a mile of running under full power in Pearl Harbor. Some of the ships that the Japanese air force sank were still sticking up out of the water, and I was having visions of hitting one and becoming a monument myself. The plane shuddered violently as the suction broke, and this giant bird rose slowly into the heavens. What a wonderful, exhilarating feeling that was.

The cabins were only semi—pressurized. Children screamed all the way across, and my ears hurt enough to scream with them. Parents cried, we all bitched, and as usual we got there anyway, the Navy way. Landing in Frisco Bay at night was beautiful. The sparkling lights from the city skyline and from the shore washed the rigors of the flight away. Except for the hissing sound of a large moving body settling into the water, it was eerily silent. We were home. Good old U.S.A. soil.

In Alameda, California, the navy put all the personnel ready for discharge in a section called Splinter City. It was easy to see how it got its name—old, dilapidated, and drafty rooms, more like halls, to sleep in.

One of my buddies back at Lualualei had warned me that pressure would be put on us to reenlist or sign up for the reserves. "Don't, under any circumstances, sign *anything*. You will be threatened, put in a place that is uncomfortable, and pressured. Don't sign anything," he warned. I remembered his advice, and for almost two weeks I was grilled, pressured, screamed at, and threatened—but I didn't sign up. It was like an inquisition. Were these guys Spanish? Did my records show them I was a Marano? Two of them standing over me, obviously enjoying their work, kept trying to break me down.

"We have ways of keeping you here a long time, don't you want to go home?"

"Yes," I answered, "but I won't sign up again, I did my time." I kept looking around for the Grand Inquisitor in his scarlet robes to point his finger at me and shout, "Convert or die."

"Did your time, shit," the recruiters said. "You're going to sign or stay here until you're an old man." When were they going to put me on the rack?

This grilling kept up for two hours each day for more than a week, and then suddenly my discharge orders came through. The only fond memory from that place came from the loudspeakers in the mess hall. Vaughn Monroe singing "Racing with the Moon."

When the Korean War broke out, my buddies who did sign up in the reserves, under duress. were drafted and went back to war. Many of them did not return. George Feldman, whom I later met in New York, had a different story about signing up. He was called when the Korean War broke out and was told to settle his civilian affairs, leave his job, or sell his business. You can imagine how he felt after putting in two years already. As luck would have it, when he arrived at the induction center, the officer was his old chief. The chief took George into a small room, had a chat about old times, stamped his record "rejected" and George went home to try and retrieve the business he had just sold. Some of the inducted men died in combat. Some, like George, got away easily. You bet it's arbitrary.

Russ, another seaman named Jeff who we needed to help pay for the trip we planned, and I hired a private car and driver to take us across country to the East Coast. It was cheaper than train or bus, and the driver, although not someone I would play cards with, seemed decent enough. The trip, when I first enlisted, going to the West Coast by troop train was difficult. Two days before we hit 'Frisco the porters said they had run out of food and began charging us for what Uncle Sam had already paid for. We fought and scrambled over one another to pay for scraps of food. A car sounded better. We would be in control, I thought.

Going home now, these car drivers really had our number. We were young, eager to get home, and had money in our pockets—and they got it. Two days out we got a song and dance that he needed another twenty—five bucks from each of us because he had figured wrong, and so it went. We were cold driving over the Rocky Mountains and couldn't keep the ice off the windshields, so we filled a bag with salt at a restaurant, wet it down, and kept stopping to rub the outside of the window with wet salt. We slept in the car two of the four nights and five days it took us to get to the East Coast.

Just outside of Davenport, Iowa, in a snowstorm, we were amazed to see a young woman hitchhiking. She was standing next to a large trunk, wearing only a flowered silk dress with her thumb stuck out. The driver seemed frightened, he didn't want to stop, but Russ and I were intrigued. *Had he seen this same girl standing there on his last trip*, I wondered? *Is this the sister siren of the mermaid who intoxicates all men in their ships at sea as they pass, then drowns them?* We asked where she was going and her answer was, "East." There wasn't room for the trunk so she left it, and everything in it, right by the side of the road.

Her name was May, and she was indeed a siren. Her body radiated heat and she kept the entire car warm. "What the hell are you doing in a silk dress, hitchhiking in a snow storm?" I asked.

"The sheriff threw me out cause I was sellin' it. I ran out of money and had to. I don't do that as a rule, only when I'm down on my luck." She never answered my question about the silk dress.

As the trip progressed she went from lap to lap and certainly kept us livelier than we would otherwise have been. At one point my questions annoyed her, and she asked, "What are you anyway, some kind of lawyer?" I assured her I wasn't. "What are you, a Jew?"

Ah, the magic word. "Yes," I answered her, and could see that she never expected me to say yes and was immediately sorry she had asked that way. She knew she had stepped over the invisible line. After that, when we did stop for the night, she would come close to me and hit my leg with her hand, letting me know that she would be with me. Foolish me, I wouldn't have any of it. Our greasy driver wanted her, but she wouldn't have any of him.

Jeff was dropped off somewhere in the Chicago area, and we had more room in the car. By this time the driver showed his true colors. He was a lush and had bottles tucked everywhere. I took over the driving until he looked stable again. I didn't want to do this any more than was necessary because I had no civilian license. Russ and May our human stove, were snuggling in the back, lying stretched out on the seat under a blanket. When I drove I could see every move of their bodies in the rearview mirror. Each time it looked like Russ was about to enter her, I hit the brakes four or five times quickly, and they would disengage. One time Russ rolled right onto the floor. May thought it was a riot, Russ was pissed, but I couldn't stop doing it. I guess if I didn't have her, I didn't want Russ to have her either.

We left the car and driver, who was still asking for more money, on the New York side of the Lincoln Tunnel. We found our way to a subway, dragging our duffel bags through the snow, and went to Forest Hills in Queens, where my aunt lived. Russ hadn't been in a subway before, and he was in awe of all the people milling and pushing around him. We were two sailors and a girl, rumpled and tired, with two duffel bags stuffed full, trying to find space in the subway car.

In January 1948, New York was under two feet of snow from the heaviest storm in its history, and nothing was moving on the surface except a few cabs. We desperately wanted a shower, clean beds, and sleep. Getting out of the subway at the Forest Hills station at 108th Street and Queens Boulevard, we climbed over a large snow pile, got into a cab and asked to be taken to the nearest hotel. The cab driver took us on a twenty—minute, wheel-spinning ride. The cab came to a halt sliding sideways against a snow mound in front of the hotel. Stepping out into the snow bank, I glanced up the street and saw that were only two blocks from where we had hailed him. My learning curve was moving up. I paid the driver and gave him a quarter tip and he held his palm open with the coin in it, disdain written all over his face. I reached over and took the quarter from him and put it back in my pocket. He gave me what I was to label in the future, a New York finger.

We were at an elegant place called the Forest Hills Inn. I learned later that their policy was no Jews or blacks. I certainly wouldn't have put myself in this position had I known about it ahead of time. The man at the desk looked at me and said, "We have no rooms available." *Now how the hell did he know I was a Jew? Did I look different than Russ? Or maybe he thought Russ was the Jew. I might as well be wearing an armband with a star on it,* I thought. "What are you talking about?" I said. "There are people being registered as we speak. What kind of treatment is this for servicemen who have been fighting for you?" I shouted, knowing that they wouldn't dare call the police. It worked.

We were taken to a closed—off portion of the hotel with flaking paint and little heat. I was happy to get anything at this point. As we were signing in, May kept hitting my leg. One of us had to be with her, but my feelings were confused. Why would she want to be with me when even the damn hotel didn't want me there? Russ and May logged in as mister and misses.

The next morning I looked up my aunt Esta's phone number under her new name, Mazarin. I called and told her I would be over. We said good-bye to May, giving her twenty bucks each so she could stay off the streets for a couple of days. It was actually sad. She had become a part of our troop. But I couldn't take her to Aunt Esta's. Esta wouldn't understand. To her sex is for having babies.

Russ and I caught a cab to Esta's place. Esta was the oldest of the Rolsky clan and a tough cookie. I remembered how she used to be—even her stance was confrontational. Arms slightly raised to the side, cocked head thrust forward. It would be a fight from the get go.

We got out of the cab in front of a very fancy apartment house, went into the lobby, found Aunt Esta's apartment number on her mail box, got into the elevator, and pressed five. If I thought this was pretty high living for a Rolsky, you should have seen Russ's face. He kept mumbling "It's like in the movies, it's like in the movies." He made me uncomfortable.

Russ hailed from a small town in Massachusetts, as was evident in his New England twang. He was a pulp and paper factory worker like his father before him, and his uncles were still doing the same work. He was smart as a whip, very strong, and had a strikingly handsome freckled face with curly hair falling down his forehead and a smile that could light up a room. His views of the world and of women in particular were astonishing. He told me a story about Janet, his high school sweetheart. They were deeply in love, inseparable, and to be married. "I went over to Janet's house on Friday evening, after I got paid, and we usually went out from there," Russ told me. "She came running toward me, as I walked up the stoop, and threw herself into my arms. I loved it when she did that. I caught her and squeezed her tight and she farted. I couldn't look at her after that. We broke up."

" Russ are you telling me that...what are you saying? That because she farted you broke up?".

"I couldn't look at her after that," Russ said.

"Don't you think she has a digestive system, too? That's a crazy thing to do. You even caused it, you squeezed her," I said.

"I know, but once she farted, I lost all feeling for her."

Lucky for her, I thought. *What if they had married and then he found out she was a live person?*

I rang Aunt Esta's doorbell, and there she was, hugging me and asking if I was hungry and totally ignoring Russ. I stopped and introduced them, but Esta went right on talking about her family and her son, my cousin Duste. His real name was Sanford, after his biological dad, Seymour. Everyone called him Duste (he used an e instead of the usual y at the end of his name) because he always acted like a cowboy character. He wore boots and a cowboy hat to school, so the name stuck. Duste's real father was a fireman who died before he was born, so the only father he knew was Jules Mazarin. When Duste's real father died, Esta dumped Duste with my family for a couple of years, when we were in New York on Post Avenue. During that time, he transferred his affections to my mother. Esta took him back to live with her, but I don't think he ever got over my mom. We were never really friendly after that. I think he always resented me because I had the mother he wanted.

Esta was a very good cook. She had to be to satisfy Jules. I didn't know how lucky I was that he was out of town on a sales trip. She fed us the kind of food we had been dreaming about for two years. As I think of it now it really wasn't the food—London broil, baked potatoes, and broccoli. It was the plates, the silverware, the cloth napkins, and the service. We had been standing in line jostling and walking past steel food tables so long that this seemed like a dream.

It was a short-lived dream for Russ. As the day wore on, it was obvious that Esta didn't want him to stay the night. Was it because he wasn't Jewish? I took him aside and said, "Get a room back at the hotel and I'll meet you in the morning. We'll take a train to Worcester, visit your people, and then I will continue on to Bangor. I can't leave right now—I need to set my plans with my aunt about coming back here to live."

Russ would have none of it. "I'm headed home *now* Murry, if you want to stay that's okay." And Russ, dragging his duffel, was gone. The break with my navy years was sudden and complete. I wanted to go with him. We had bonded together for the past eighteen months. He was closer to me than my Aunt Esta but I needed a place to stay in New York. I let him go without a fuss.

• • •

I bumped into Russ one more time, five years later in front of Grand Central Station. "Russ, what the hell are you doing here?" I exclaimed in my excitement at seeing him again. I was dressed in a suit and tie. He had never seen me dressed up. He didn't want to talk to me. There was no sign of the old friendship in his eyes, just suspicion, anger, and a look of jealousy from what he perceived as my success. He just walked on. I watched him go East on 42nd Street as I tried to deal with my own feelings of disappointment, rejection and anger. at his attitude.

• • •

I stayed with Aunt Esta for a few nights and made arrangements to come back and live with her, Jules, and Duste so I could go to school in New York on the GI Bill. She was to be paid thirteen dollars a month for food, since Jules would not increase her food allowance. Then I took the train home to see Dad and Bob.

Aunt Esta wasn't keen on having me live there, but since Mom took in Duste years earlier she couldn't fuss too much. Duste wasn't happy about my sharing a tiny room with him, and Jules just wanted to see what the hell would happen when we were all crowded into one small apartment. He wasn't around that much, so it didn't impact on him.

108th Street and Queens Boulevard, called the Village or Continental Avenue, was the great gathering place for teens looking for fun or trouble. There was a drug store and a subway on the corner and shops of all kinds on both sides of the street from Queens Blvd. down to Austin Street, where my uncle Ben had his store two blocks up.

Uncle Ben had settled in Forest Hills with his wife, Rose, as well as my Aunt Esta and Jules and Aunt Freda with her husband, Lou. All were doing well and had kids of their own. Ben had two sons, Richard and Gary. Alfreda had a daughter, Gail, and two sons, Mark and Lloyd. The family was growing and, still unknown to me, I would eventually live in the homes of each of them, in their basements.

Slowly, the Rolsky clan under different names was gathering in Forest Hills. Ben changed his name from Rolsky to Dorsey, Alfreda married a Handelsman (now changed to Hanes), and Esta Rolsky of course had married a Mazarin. My name, Handler, had itself been shortened from Oxenhandler by my

101

father. No full name was left from our past history. No one kept a record of our European roots. We were all too busy surviving and blending in.

• • •

It looked like another fun night at the Mazarin apartment, where I now lived. Jules, the son of a bitch, just walked into the living room stark naked. Fine furniture, wall—to—wall wool carpeting, beautiful amenities for dining—this was a classy place. But it was a home that lacked civility. Marilyn, Jules's sexy sixteen—year—old daughter from a previous marriage, was visiting for a few days. We were about to eat dinner, and here was Jules coming to the table in his birthday suit. The man was in his late forties, with a jaw that put him a close relative to a bulldog. When he sat down he complained that the chair was cold. I was hoping that the cane seats, which sometimes had slivers, would stick into something down there that would really make him jump, but no such luck.

Marilyn hid her face in her hands. Duste said, "Awe for Chrissakes, dad."

Esta said, "Pussy cat." This was her term of endearment for Jules.

I didn't comment because I was torn between shame, laughter, and hunger. I knew if I laughed at him my life would be more miserable than usual.

"This is the natural way to live. Why don't people leave their clothes off and be comfortable?" Jules announced.

"Dad, it isn't right that you come to the table naked and with your daughter here," Duste said.

"Pussy cat, why don't you just go in and slip a robe on," Esta said.

"Aw, shut up and get me a napkin to sit on," Jules replied. Esta was always the one he turned on.

We ate with Jules dining naked, his daughter peeking at him now and then. When the meal ended we all got up and left the table. His nakedness forgotten, Jules went into the bedroom and put on a robe.

It was one thing for Jules to stand in the bathroom each morning shaving naked with the door open. It was quite another for him to go naked during the day with everyone around. He apparently had reached a new plateau in self—indulgence. Jules was losing his youth and seemed unhappy with Esta. He wanted excitement and late nights out at bars, Esta didn't understand that kind of life.

When I went to pee in the morning, I had to do it with Jules shaving and often commenting on my urine color. "Esta," he shouted, "something's wrong with this kid. His piss is too yellow. Better take him to a doctor. Hey kid, gettin any nookie? I'll take you to someone like I did Duste, just to get you started."

Jules had taken Duste to a whore when he was sixteen years old. I guess he thought that was the way to make a man out of him. Duste told me he didn't enjoy any of it. "The gal was nice enough," Duste said, "and she talked to me like I was her kid brother, but it just wasn't any fun and it hurt when we did it." I couldn't figure that one out. How the hell *could* it be fun at sixteen with your own father taking you into a strange woman, paying her for sex while he waits outside the door. I'm glad the son of a bitch wasn't my old man. Come to think of it, mine wouldn't have spent the money.

In sixteen forty one another Jules Mazarin, an Italian, became Cardinal of France. He took over from Cardinal

Richelieu. If this was Uncle Jules' family line it did explain some of his brutish actions.

Unknown to Jules or anyone else, I had connected with a little redhead who was a Village hangout. I had been talking with a few of the guys on the corner one evening, and I sensed someone was watching me. This funny little redhead, who had been staring at me for a while, walked over and introduced herself. "Hi, I'm Red," she said and suggested we have a soda. We met a couple of more times on the corner, took walks together, and one night she led me up 108th Street to a tiny wooded area with a bench right next to a large apartment house. She had been this way before.

Upbringing didn't stop me this time. She did it all for me. It's a good thing it was dark and she couldn't see the color of my face. She didn't have intercourse with me but took me in her well educated hand and expertly jerked me off. She was, if not a full—course meal, a much—appreciated appetizer. Red made no demands, she just wanted to please. She kept me sane for the next couple of months and eventually did serve wholesome, full—course dinners.

When I left for school each morning it was a blessing. I had been accepted at The Franklin Institute of Art located in a penthouse on Park Avenue. The work was hard but it forced me to hunker down and learn. There were some pretty women students there. One gal Kate, used to corner me on the narrow balcony overlooking Park Avenue and push her knee between my legs asking me to take her out but when she heard I didn't have a car or any money either she lost interest and I lost a knee. "How about taking me to a movie Murry?" she would ask. Pick me up at six and we can have dinner," Kate continued talking as she pinned me to the side of the balcony with her educated leg between mine. "Sorry Kate, I don't have a car or a kopek to my name—how about your place," I asked. She pulled back, looked at me and shook her head in disbelief and took off.

Jules always wanted a son who was a whoring, fighting, womanizing son of a bitch just like himself, and Duste didn't cut it. He tried hard; he wanted to please Jules. Duste was handsome and had plenty of pretty girls he was bedding, but his heart just wasn't in the rest of it. Jules had a son, Jimmy, Marilyn's brother, by his previous marriage, but Jimmy was small and quiet. Jules didn't have his gladiator.

I came home late one evening, looking like hell. My head had a huge lump and cut on it from standing up under an open cabinet door at school. The hem of my overcoat was covered with food that had spilled in the cafeteria and had dried all crusted. Jules glanced at me and said, "What the hell happened to you?"

I instantly made up the kind of story I knew he would love. "I met some guys at the pool hall. One of them was a tough guy and I didn't get out of his way fast enough. He hit me on the head with the rack and knocked me out cold. When I woke up everyone was gone. That's where I got this lump."

"What's that crap all over your coat?" Jules asked, not really questioning my story.

"We were drinking, and I got a little sick" I said.

Jules's face began to take on the look of a man who is seeing his messiah arriving. I was what he wanted Duste and Jimmy to be. For a while, there wasn't much I could do wrong. Anytime either Esta or Duste criticized me, Jules stuck up for me. It was a nasty bit of deception but necessary for survival.

"Pussy cat, what the hell is this?" asked Esta. Answering her own question, she shouted, "It's lipstick on your undershorts! You bastard!"

"What the hell are you talking about? Let me see that," Jules said as he came into the laundry area. He examined the shorts carefully and said, "Well honey, there's nothing to worry about, it's not on the front of the shorts," and he fell into a fit of laughter at his own wit. His laughter was truly infectious and the situation so ridiculous that even Esta kept sliding into body giggles as she continued to berate him. I was to find out that this was nothing new—it happened again and again. If Esta pressed him too hard, she knew he would take a walk.

Jules had the first television set we ever saw. It was made by some guy named Joe who lived on the other side of the apartment house. It was a huge piece of furniture with a tiny screen near the top. We all gathered around it to watch ball games. Every time a tube blew, Jules called Joe to come down and fix it. And he did, over and over again. Jules liked watching boxing, and when a match was coming on TV he made a big deal of it. He insisted Esta serve hot dogs on rolls with sauerkraut, popcorn, and soda, on demand. When she didn't he raised hell, and when she did he raised hell about something else. I ate the goddamned hot dogs and popcorn, watched his goddamned fights, and kept out of his way while I worked to get out of his house.

I came home from school early one day. Aunt Esta was in Maine visiting the family and wasn't due back until the next day. Jules was packing his bags. There was nothing unusual about that, he was always traveling. He kept asking me to talk to him, help him down with his bags and "say good-bye downstairs when the cab comes, kid." He never did that before. He could have cared less about saying good—bye to me, so I just shrugged it off as another of his oddities.

When I came home from school the next day, Esta was back from Maine. She was crying and shouting at me, "Why didn't you stop him, why didn't you stop him from leaving?" It immediately threw my mind back to Bob, as a baby, rolling under my cot. "Didn't you see him, didn't you see him?" Esta as a young girl, shouting back then, too. It took me a moment to respond as a nineteen—year—old and not a three—year—old.

"Why should I stop him from going on a trip? As if I could," I answered flippantly.

"He took his clothes, his bags, his jewelry, emptied out all his drawers. He's gone," she sobbed. How the hell am I supposed to know what was going on between these two? *Is she right*, I thought? *Does someone really just leave like that? When you die you leave like that.*

She should be grateful the prick was gone. He used to stay out until all hours without calling, coming home drunk, lipstick on his underwear. She should have been glad, happy even.

The bastard really was gone. He left Duste, who loved him, his wife who, well whatever the relationship, she *was* his wife. He left, as we later found out, for a young redhead with three kids of her own. Years later Jules left her as well. The last time I heard about him was when Duste went to his funeral.

Esta remained alone for the rest of her long life, dying at ninety—three, in a nursing home in Florida near her only child. I don't know if there was a funeral or memorial for her. I wasn't even notified. My uncle Ben called me afterwards and told me.

• • •

I needed a job to supplement my GI Bill allotment of seventy—five bucks a month. After paying room and board to Aunt Esta, subway fare, and art supplies, I was broke. I couldn't even take myself, much less a girl, to the movies. I got to know the girl in the Loew's movie ticket booth on Queens Boulevard, and she would let me in for free a half hour after the last show had already started. I met her while I was working nights at a nearby soda counter, and she invited me to come around to the movie after 9:30. I was too dumb to realize that she might be interested in me. I just went to the movies for free and longed to know how the films began.

Not being very sophisticated about job placement agencies and no one to turn to for advice, I chose the largest office building in New York City to begin my job search. I took the elevator to the top office floor of the Empire State Building and walked my way down, knocking on doors and asking for work. "What kind of work are you looking for?" one of the kinder men asked.

"I want to be an artist," I responded, honest and right to the point.

"Can you do illustrations like these stockings on our package?" the man asked.

I looked closely at what he was showing me and thought it was a photograph. I was embarrassed, but I learned a lesson from it. When the next person asked me what I wanted to do I just said "anything," and that's what I got. I swept floors, emptied wastebaskets, packed pants in cartons, jerked sodas— everything for $1.75 an hour and happy to get it.

When I was accepted at the Franklin Institute of Art. I came to them in the same stumbling way I went for jobs, with no research and no way to judge the quality of the school. I looked up the address in the phone book and went right to them. It didn't cross my mind that one might be better than the other, nor did I realize the importance of this once—in—a—lifetime opportunity. All the schools asked to see my portfolio. I didn't have one and wouldn't have known how to put one together anyway. At the Franklin Institute they saw this hick coming. The GI Bill assured them of their tuition, and that was prime. Not that it wasn't an accredited school and doing some good work. In fact, I got some good training and a fine base for my later art education.

Late at night, almost every night, when Esta and Duste were asleep and Jules was on the road selling. I would sit at a small drawing table at the foot of my bed, doing schoolwork and making illustration samples. If it took hard work, well, that was one of the few things I did know how to do.

• • •

I made the first of several moves from Esta's house to my aunt Alfreda, a follower of Mary Baker Eddy, and her husband, Lou and their three kids, Lloyd, Mark, and Gail. It was a wonderful, Tudor—style house just off 108th Street in Forest Hills. I actually got a bedroom upstairs for a while, but Lou snored so heavily that the walls vibrated and I couldn't sleep. I went to live in the basement, painted ocean murals on the walls with whales swimming around. I considered it an omen when I woke up, swung my feet over the side of the cot I slept on, and was shocked by cold water that came midway to my calves. My shoes were floating. All my stuff that was left leaning against the wall—paintings, paper, rulers—were ruined with the flooded basement. I couldn't pay for my own place, so it was this or the poor house. I kept all things off the floor after that and put my hand over the side before I stepped out of bed each morning. Yes, there were more floods.

I took my showers upstairs because there wasn't one in the basement. I have a habit of singing or whistling a lot of the time, especially while in the shower. I don't know why, but the Lord's Prayer was on my mind that morning. I must have heard it on the radio and it stayed with me. I sang it loud and clear several times, and as I stepped out of the shower there sat my cousin Lloyd on a stool in front of the sink, with an angelic look on his face.

"Lloyd, what are you doing in the bathroom with me?" I asked.

Never losing his angelic look, Lloyd said, "Mom sent me up to listen."

Aha, I was the religious moment of the day. I remembered that and sang the Lord's Prayer when I needed the attention of my aunt. Lou didn't fall for that stuff.

My little cousin Gail took ballet lessons. She was a beautiful child with graceful limbs and long blond hair, and I started painting a portrait of her in her tutu. The portrait, though never properly finished, brought Gail and me closer together in a bond that has lasted for more than fifty years. Her brothers, Mark and Lloyd, were sent away to private schools as young men, and were never as close as Gail and I.

One particular week I was babysitting all three children while Aunt Alfreda and Uncle Lou were on a cruise in the Caribbean. Mark was standing on a desktop, trying to reach something and he fell, hitting his arm on an open drawer. Both of his arm bones were broken about halfway between the wrist and the elbow. I was hesitant, but Mark insisted that I call a Christian Science elder from their church. "This is what my folks would want," he said. The elder came and sat with Mark, praying through the night, while I watched his arm swell, turning blue, then darker and blacker. In the early morning hours I had had enough. I called Uncle Ben, who owned the dress shop on Austin Street and lived just a short drive away.

"This healer isn't healing, Uncle Ben, and I don't want the responsibility all alone. I'm afraid Mark will lose his arm," I told him.

He was there within twenty minutes, told the elder to scram, called the doctor, took Mark (who by this time was in great pain) to the hospital emergency room for x-rays, had the arm set, and was back home before the sun came up. He then put a call through to the cruise ship that Al and Lou were on and told them the story. They said he did the right thing, and they didn't come home for another five days.

6

Enid

It was Friday, and the lights from the store windows in the Village cast a holiday glow over the crowd. Three guys I had seen hanging around before but I didn't know, were palavering with coins in their hands. I knew the signs, and as I moved in closer to maybe catch what was happening I found that I was right. They needed another dollar and change to buy a pint.

"Hey guys my name is Murry. I'm new around here and would like to join you. Is there something I can contribute to?" I asked.

A few seconds of looks and whispers and Dave, the blond one, stepped in my direction. He couldn't have been more than seventeen, and although I was only two years older he seemed like a kid. The other guys might be eighteen, but they better have IDs.

"We're a little short of cash to buy a pint of Southern Comfort", he said. "We know where there's a party going on and want to get some booze and crash it. If you're interested, we need another dollar and sixty seven cents."

I handed over two bucks and waved off the change. One of them went into the liquor store and bought the pint. "Where's the party?" I asked.

We walked down Continental Avenue, away from Queens Boulevard, taking swigs from the bottle as we went. We crossed Austin Street and headed toward the Gardens. The party was in the Garden section of Forest Hills, a very fancy area. The famous Forest Hills tennis courts were in here. As we walked along the streets in the dark punctuated by light from the street lamps, I began to notice how big the houses were—small plots of land immaculately landscaped with huge two—storied houses lining the street.

Even at night the gigantic Tudor house that was our destination looked impressive. A dark red brick first floor, with wonderful stained wood patterns showing through the white plaster exterior on the second floor. We could hear the noise and music, and the excitement sent shivers through me as we picked our way along the carefully laid stones of the Japanese—style walkway softly illuminated by light coming from the windows. I had never crashed anything before. In Bangor, Jews don't crash, they get crashed. But these people were all Jews. There was something comforting about this. *Would I have to confine myself to associating only with other Jews to be comfortable,* I wondered? I'll be damned if I'll let myself be forced into this limiting life style. I won't let religions do this to me, but I was beginning to understand why most of my family and friends did just that. It was total acceptance not rejection.

I was preparing myself for a quick exit in case we ran into trouble from the parents, but these guys I was with were good. They walked without hesitation right through the front door and into the high school crowd with me following. The hostess showed only slight hesitation as we walked past her. We were a bit older (at least I was) than the other guys at the party, and she seemed to like that.

Looking around, there wasn't much of interest until I heard a well—modulated young woman's voice and turned to see a very proper young thing, sitting erect, conscious of herself and her audience of young men. She looked about seventeen or eighteen years old, with a pretty face and a great body. But what really attracted me to her was her carriage and poise. She was interesting. I moved through the circle in front of her, sat right next to her, and joined the conversation. As the hours went by the group whittled down to just the two of us, but I don't think either one of us noticed the others leaving.

Even after she invited me to her sweet sixteen party, I didn't bolt. I was petrified, but smitten. We spent the entire evening talking together, and it was wonderful. When it was time to go home I didn't know proper manners—when you monopolize a girl's evening you're supposed to escort her home, even if you didn't bring her. And that's what she asked me: "Aren't you going to take me home, Murry?"

I suddenly felt trapped. What was I doing with this fifteen—year—old kid who seemed so adult and in control? She was jail—bait. Embarrassment and confusion contributed to my saying "No, I'm sorry I can't take you home."

Enid didn't blanch, but the "look," which I would come to recognize, was inescapable even then.

The next morning was Sunday, and at breakfast, I told my Aunt Esta that I had met the girl I would marry, but she was only fifteen and I had to wait until she grew up. The strange thing is that Aunt Esta took me seriously. She believed me. I asked her about escorting Enid home and although she didn't seem too certain (she came from the same place I did, so how would she know etiquette), she agreed with Enid that it was the right thing to do. Guilt at not taking her home, attraction to the forbidden, and my memory of this sweet girl the night before made the phone call to apologize inevitable. Enid didn't stay angry with me for long. Her voice was a bit cold at first, but that didn't last. We started to see each other. However, I declined Enid's invitation to her sweet sixteen, birthday party because, as I told my aunt, "She's just too young to get started with."

Enid's folks were middle—class, educated people. Her father, Solomon Ostrov, was an attorney and her mother, Fran Ostrov, was a schoolteacher. My strengths were in interpreting body language, glances, innuendo, voice changes and watching my ass. All these were highly developed and were a counter weight for my lack of education and culture. In my ignorance I didn't feel intimidated by them. I didn't even recognize the social strata difference. Sol and Fran were not happy about me, but they knew and respected Enid. She was the apple of their eyes.

Listening to the news on the radio was the closest thing I remember to cultural activities growing up in Bangor. My family didn't have music or art appreciation, and there was no television then. The rest of the Jewish kids in town took music lessons, so I took clarinet and saxophone and wondered why we wasted our money on things none of us were interested in. We were poor and owned little of value except a great deal of personal pride that mom instilled in us. I had visited other friends' homes and understood that there were better ways and nicer things to reach for. I was a sponge ready for absorbing when I met Enid and her family, but I also carried a lot of my own heavy baggage. On our third date, Enid asked me why I didn't kiss her goodnight. God, it was embarrassing. My fathers words still rang in my head: "Don't touch the girls."

• • •

It wasn't so easy being in love with a well—off chick. I couldn't afford to take her to her high school prom, so I watched someone else take her. Enid had a steady boyfriend from a well—off family before I came along, and he was pressing to stay around. I needed time to build something into my life, but I wasn't going to get it by staying in school. So I left a full—time curriculum to get a job and do school at night.

My cousin Duste had a job in the mailroom at the J. Walter Thompson Advertising Agency in Manhattan, courtesy of a Forest Hills neighbor who had a fairly high position there. Duste got me an interview with an art director named Mike whom he had become friendly with while delivering his mail. Mike got me a job as a messenger with Lester Rossin Art Studio, which he used as a supplier, and my career was off and running. Literally.

I was able to buy Enid a high school graduation gift of gold antique earrings, which she wears to this day. When I see them on her, I still feel proud. When I saw her leaving for her prom with another guy but wearing my earrings, I felt like shit. The earrings set me back fifty bucks and I had to not only eat hot dogs for lunch for a month but walk from New York to Forest Hills with my bad legs at day's end because I didn't have a dime for the subway. If that's why my feet and legs are so bad today, I still think it was worth it.

The difficulty of separating in the evenings was tearing Enid and me apart. Saying good—night at her front door, just the brush of our hands would create hours of longing as I lay alone in my cot in one of my aunt's basements. Enid had very quickly become the center of my emotional world. All my love, all my feelings were open to her. I trusted her knowing she wouldn't betray these feelings.

I think I was living right around the corner from Enid in Uncle Ben's and Aunt Rose's house by this time. I will never forget the day they left for vacation. They mothballed the house as usual when they left, forgetting that I was living in the basement. What a miserable week of trying to sleep that was. There weren't any windows in the basement, so I slept on the living room floor with the windows wide open. It was still impossible. I tasted mothballs in my food for a month, no matter what I ate.

Enid's house was on the next block with all attached homes. Some set back a bit more than others to break what would have been a monotonous line of porches. All the tiny front lawns were situated to the right of a very narrow cement path. Up, one step from the sidewalk then three more at the deck, which was only six feet wide and twenty eight feet across the entire front of the house. They were kept immaculate. People talked from one deck to another as they sat and relaxed on evenings and weekends.

I couldn't support a wife at this time in my life. Enid was now in college, and I was still broke, even with a full—time job, working weekends at another, and going to school at night. Paying room and board and making illustration samples took all my money and time. It was cruel and painful being apart. Nature was not having its way.

At the Ostrov dinner table, which Enid invited me to join more and more, her father always wore a tie and a shirt, with cufflinks. He was a formal kind of guy and these were his clothes from the office. He didn't change into anything different until he went to bed. I usually wore a T—shirt with a hole in it somewhere. That's how my shirts were. I also had a habit of humming to myself or whistling without realizing it. Sol's conversation with me consisted of "you shouldn't hum at the table." Don't do this, don't do that. As an attorney, he was used to telling people what to do. I had crawled out from under shit like this when I left my father's house and would have preferred to develop a relationship with Sol as a friend, but I didn't know how and neither did he. So we stayed at arm's length for many years after my marriage to his daughter. Thinking about it now, it seems he wanted a son but didn't understand how to go about it. I was twenty, a veteran of World War II, and I did not want another father figure.

Sol was about six feet tall with very large hands and muscular thighs and legs. He had been on his college basketball team as a young man, but showed no residue of his former athleticism. He had an olive complexion, white sideburns, a slight bald spot on top of his head, and always the shadow of a beard. His evenings were spent in front of the TV, playing chess moves by himself, or out with Fran at a client's house. He could have doubled for Abdel Gamal Nasser of Egypt. He came from a rough neighborhood in the Bronx and sounded like it. His father, Sam, had been a tailor and his brother Abe did a little bootlegging on the side during prohibition. Actually the bootlegging was out the window. Let me explain. Sol's mother had a small barrel on two chains hanging out of her bathroom window, over the alley, so no one would see it. It was filled with bathtub booze and only Abe was strong enough pull it up. Abe was unusually strong and the first time I met him in Fran and Sol's house he immediately took me into the kitchen where the phone was and tore the Queens phone book in half so I would know what he was about. I don't know why Sol was furious with him, phone books were free then. It's a good thing he was strong because he wasn't too swift upstairs. Not a dumb man, just totally uneducated and absolutely no couth. Sol's sister Jean was a schoolteacher. A wiry, coarse woman well aware of her homely features, who could probably have torn the phone book in half herself but had a bit more decorum. The first time I met her she complained to me about her husband Norman's philandering. I hadn't even met Norman yet but this was Jean telling me who she was. Norman was a shoe store salesman who wore pin srtiped suits and could have been a car salesman or fit any of that mold. Norman liked women and Jean couldn't keep him home. Lena and Sam, Sol's parents sent one son and one daughter to college. Abe was left out. I thought they made the right choices. Abe didn't.

Enid's mom, Fran, was another story—a small, pretty, woman who emanated warmth, love, and caring. Almost every time I went to Enid's house Fran was knitting. Her hands never stopped working on some piece of clothing for someone in the family. She was always listening and giving advice in a manner that was totally acceptable. Fran was my liaison to Sol. Sometimes, now, in the evenings, when I glance over at Enid, I see Fran's movements and mannerisms. I miss both my mother

119

and father—in—law, and Enid's actions are a wonderful reminder that they are still with us.

The closet to the right in the entry, in Enid's house, had been changed to a powder room with a small corner bowl and a toilet. Straight ahead and to the left, the stairs lead up to the three bedrooms and bath. To the right of the stairs was the open living room, dining room and kitchen. To the left, in back of the kitchen door, once you were inside, was another door that led to a finished basement. That's where Enid and I spent our time alone. We experimented with and explored each other's bodies. We were so young, so sweetly and innocently in love. When Enid was eighteen and I was twenty-two, we consummated a union that would become more than fifty wonderful years together and still going. After that we knew (and so did Enid's mother who sensed everything) that marriage wasn't far ahead.

This was a difficult time for me, and my father was not supportive. He had a very strange methodology of helping. When we were at a family affair, like a bar mitzvah or a wedding, he would make certain to meet me in the men's room and slip me a twenty—dollar bill. It was always done surreptitiously. I accepted his money for a while because he wouldn't listen to me when I tried to refuse, even though I needed the money. Eventually, I started calling it potty money. With a label like that it couldn't be good.

My family, all around me now in New York, didn't even try to get to know the Ostrovs. The Ostrovs must have wondered what kind of people their daughter was marrying into. My mother would have taken all of Enid's family to her bosom, but she was gone. Like everything else in life, I had to do it myself, and eventually I earned Sol and Fran's love and trust.

Early mornings, before Enid took the train to school, we would meet for breakfast. Enid got ten dollars a week for allowance. This was as much as was left of my fourteen dollars each week on salary after taxes. She paid for both our breakfasts. I wouldn't have eaten breakfast otherwise, and she knew it. Enid was embarrassed to pay for me. Women didn't pay for men in those days, it was unheard of. She wanted to slip the money under the table. I insisted that she was treating and should pay without feeling ashamed. Her embarrassment and what was left of my pride collided at almost every breakfast. This did not go on for long. Our need to be together intensified. Enid, who loved reading and being a student, decided to leave college, find a job, wait for my career to take off, and *then* go back to school. She had spent only one year at Adelphi College when she left. No greater love.

Three children and nine years later Enid finally did go back to school, taking her undergraduate degree at Queens College, her master's from the School of Physicians and Surgeons Public Health Division at Columbia University and started a long and successful career of her own. I couldn't have done what she did.

I didn't have money for an engagement ring and Sadye, my dad's new wife, offered me a small diamond she had. I jumped at it. Fifty bucks for the setting was about my limit. One of my most embarrassing moments was coming to Enid's house and seeing a couple of friends of the Ostrovs sitting on the couch in the living room, looking through a jeweler's glass at Enid's engagement ring. I knew it was not a very good stone, and the man looking up at me with this ridiculous plastic magnifier in his eye tried to say something nice about it, but couldn't. I was mortified and furious. Who the hell did they think they were. Enid and I didn't care if the damn thing was glass—it got the job done. It took me a while to get over that one.

The wedding was totally out of our hands. We were asked little if anything and were overruled at every turn by Enid's parents. I couldn't offer any alternatives. I had no money to translate into power.

"What kind of a wedding would you children like?" Fran asked.

"We would prefer it simple and small," Enid and I would say, *almost* in unison.

"Sol needs to invite all his clients to get back some of the gifts we have been giving to their kids all these years," Fran gave as one of the reasons for the big show. And it *was* a big show. Our wedding was at the Belmont Plaza's Grand Ballroom in Manhattan. I actually think Enid enjoyed it. All of my family from Maine, Forest Hills, and New York City came to see Lil's firstborn get married. I think it was a combination of balm for their consciences and curiosity to see who the poor kid married. They came, they saw, they were duly impressed. I don't know how I got the nerve, but with Fran's words in my head, "Sol needs to invite all his clients to get back some of the gifts we have been giving to their kids all these years," I went from table to table, shaking hands, accepting the cash envelopes with my left hand and stuffing them into my pockets. It may have been gross (it *was* gross), but it sure helped us survive our first year of married life. My dad came with his new wife, and my heart was like a stone when I saw her beside him. I was happy for Dad when he re—married and I had held one end of the Chupah but this was a different emotion. Looking around and seeing all my

122

family in place with their correct mates except for my Mom, did something to my insides. It should have been my mother on his arm. I was not very good at hiding my feelings that day.

Discomfort with all the hoopla, my inability to control any of the ritual, made me adamant about the very few things that I could affect. "No, I *won't* wear tails," I said. God, that made me feel good. I wouldn't have worn tails even if I wanted to, because Sol wanted to and I was calling this one shot.

Enid was beautiful in her gown, and she was accustomed to handling people and situations and me. She knew how I felt and who I was, and she did her best to keep an even keel in a kind of wedding neither of us wanted. It was a beautiful wedding. The entire wall in front of the chuppah was covered with a trellis of live flowers and was magnificent. The large ballroom was resplendent with floral arrangements, ribbons, and sashes. The fifteen tables seating ten people each looked magnificent with the crystal and elegant gold—trimmed dishes. When I broke the glass under the chupah I thought my foot would go through the floor. I wish the maturity to really enjoy it all had been with me.

For our honeymoon, Uncle Sam offered to have his Cadillac waiting for us at the Bangor airport. We would drive to Lou's camp at Chemo Pond and spend our honeymoon there. Enid would have none of it. "Go into the woods and stay alone on our honeymoon?" she said. To me that seemed to be an ideal place, it was tranquil and beautiful. I could hear the sounds of the lake and the trees and smell the air filled with pine needles and ripe earth even as Sam was suggesting it. Enid, although she loved nature and places like this, was frightened. This kind of honeymoon was not in her vocabulary, and her folks thought I was crazy, too. "Go into the woods?" they exclaimed.

We went to what was familiar to Enid and her family— the Borscht circuit in the Catskill Mountains, the Jewish playground where there was superb natural beauty in the land but no peace in the worn elegance of the Nevele Country Club.

"Jesus, look at this lampshade," I said, as we unpacked our bags. "Whoever was in this room marked down every time they did it." The shade sported four vertical lines in a row, then one across diagonally. The room made me feel dirty. I wasn't comfortable in this milieu. It wasn't what I was or what Enid was. Yes, we were honeymooners, but I wanted this to be a private time together. I wanted this to be a quiet, reflective experience so we could get to know each other better. It didn't turn out that way.

Enid was late for dinner the second day at the Nevele, limping down the wide central staircase. We had been horseback riding that afternoon, and she was sore. The staircase came down to a huge lobby where everyone gathered before dinner and could see everyone else coming down. A couple of the guys, watching her limp down, started giving me elbows in the side and looks that said "you really did a job on her." I don't like a lot of people around me, even less their butting into my private life. Nothing was private here.

"For Chrissakes walk straight, don't limp," I whispered into Enid's ear as we headed for our table in the dining room. "These fools were congratulating me for beating you up sexually when they saw you limping down the stairs."

"Oh my God," Enid said, as embarrassment flushed her normally alabaster complexion. I always liked the fact that she could be embarrassed.

I had my own craziness. Enid's dad had loaned me a 35mm 3D camera to take pictures with, and I became obsessed in its use. The pictures had to be great—Enid's folks would be looking at them. Early each morning I would leave my bride's bed and go out taking pictures. On the third morning I came back to a weeping bride who couldn't understand why I preferred taking pictures to the allure of her charms. I stopped taking pictures.

During that week we watched many strange happenings on that staircase. Bob and Joanie had to leave. Joanie broke out in rashes every time he came near her. Jim, the butcher, came down on a stretcher. He threw his back out trying to add his own set of marks to his lampshade. And Joe, his wife was convinced, knew everything. He would stand at the bottom of the stairs and tell us how many angels could fit on the head of a pin, literally. We did meet one couple, Edith and Kurt Osinsky, at the Nevele who stayed lifelong friends. And that was the only good thing about it. We were very glad to get back to Queens and our new garden apartment.

• • •

"Dad, get your foot off my chair, What do you think you're doing?" Enid said.

We had just finished putting together our little three—room apartment. Sol and Fran, who bought us the prime chair for the living room, had come to visit and Sol put his foot up on the chair. I guess it was to show that he bought it and it was his to wipe his feet on. He should have known his daughter better.

She really took off on him, and then Fran took off on him. I felt offended by his actions, unable to understand what prompted him to do that. Sol was an educated man, but like me he carried a lot of early baggage of poverty and the struggle from the Bronx to Forest Hills was still apparent.

We had a wonderful first year in our apartment. I designed and built a coffee table. We cut and bound a free-form rug that curved diagonally across the living room, and we used the $4,000 cash we got at the wedding to supplement our meager earnings.

I had finished art school and was freelancing. Work was scarce, but fortunately Enid was working as well. Sometimes she was the only one who was working. We barely got by.

I went into the art studio business with a local man named Jack Edsen who I knew and Enid and I had double dated with. I don't remember what he had to offer or why I was attracted to him. My first office, Edsen—Handler Inc. was in the Seville Hotel on 28th Street, just off Madison Avenue, when I was little more than a kid. We had a spacious office on the first floor of the hotel in a former barber shop (the barber of Seville, as it were) with large glass mirrors every six feet along the wall. A barber's chair used to be in front of each of them. There were also all kinds of gold gilt rococo trim with a tile floor that looked like it belonged in a bathroom.

I represented artists and illustrators. Jack and I tried to sell their work to magazines, pocket books, and advertising agencies. We had some really good illustrators but couldn't do them justice. The big studios were wining and dining all the art buyers, and I felt that situation was wrong. It *was* wrong, but how to survive without doing it was the problem. I was brought up to think that if I worked hard and gave more than my competition, I would make it. It didn't seem to be working. The phrase "that's business" covered a lot of areas that I felt were if not illegal just not right.

One of the artists I represented was a very young, very poor Chinese girl who was married to Paul Schwar. Her father had been mayor of Canton before the communists took over. Her signature name was Di Kan, and she later rose to the top of her field in the fine art world. I got Di an assignment to paint a Chinese figure on a pocket book cover. I think it paid $175. It was the first work she had received since coming to this country and she was thrilled at the chance. I was thrilled with my 25 percent commission, too. Di, Paul, and I became friends, and we continued to work together for many years. Each time Enid gave birth, Di would do a painting especially for that child. We never dreamed they would become so valuable. Paul was a real fan of mine. He thought my pen and ink drawings were the greatest. I loved him for that. I learned of his death recently from a PBS—TV program about Di and her work.

All the artists I knew and was representing gave Enid the idea to start an art gallery out of our home in Bellerose. Di did demonstration pieces of flowers and bamboo for a select invited group. We offered them to the audience for $45 to $65, depending on the size.

"Why do you charge so much for something that only takes you fifteen minutes to do?" someone in the audience once asked.

"Fifteen minutes and thirty five years," Di would answer.

The Chinese remain students of their teacher for a lifetime, and one of Di's teachers was Chang Dai Chen, who was already famous worldwide on a level with Picasso. In fact, their estates bordered one another in South America. He came to New York for a visit to see his pupil and do some business. I was thrilled when Di invited me to meet him at the Plaza Hotel, and I took one of my best pine bonsai trees as a gift. When I arrived, Di was in the middle of washing his hair. This would be unthinkable for an American student. He had long, wispy hair and chin whiskers, just like the paintings of the old Chinese emperors we see in museums. Chang Dai Chen couldn't speak English, and the short conversation between Di, me and him, was not very satisfying. I wanted to discuss his work that I had just seen in a major show at the Hirschl Adler Gallery. The power and size of the three fifteen—foot—long scrolls hanging side by side was awsome. No such luck. I certainly felt privileged for the short time I had with him. After he left New York and went back to South America, he sent Di a photo of himself in his bonsai garden for me. I still have it. Chang Dai Chen was in his eighties then.

• • •

"Come up immediately and bring your partner. Your account is badly overdrawn." The bank was calling me at Edsen—Handler.

"Impossible," I said. "I keep the books and it is fine. You must have made a mistake."

"Look at check numbers 205 and 206." The bank manager ordered.

"I haven't reached those numbers yet," I said.

"Look at it now," he insisted.

I opened the large checkbook to those numbers buried in the two-inch depth of pages and to my astonishment the checks had been removed.

"Your partner has forged your name on those checks, come up immediately."

I put the phone down and without telling Jack the content of my discussion said, "Let's go up and see what they want."

"We will call in your loan immediately unless you sign a waiver that we are not responsible for those forged checks," the bank vice president threatened us. They closeted us in a small upstairs room over the bank and began a grilling and threatening session that lasted for hours.

"I didn't forge anything," Jack insisted.

"Shut up Jack," I said to him. "You son of a bitch, how could you do this? Why didn't you come to me?" I knew he was broke, too, and his wife made his life miserable because of it. They deserved each other.

"I didn't forge anything," Jack smirked.

I wanted to believe him, but there were the checks and my forged signatures in the same hand as his signature under mine. No one else had access to the checkbook.

"Sign, or we call in your loan," the vice president kept repeating.

"Let me call my attorney," I pleaded. If I had been sharper I would have called Sol *before* I left the studio, and he could have met us at the bank.

"Sign now or we call it in, Mr. Handler. We know you have been had by your partner, but as President of the company

129

you must sign the waiver. You're free to leave, of course, but if you do we will immediately call your loan."

I signed the waiver, left the bank, told Jack my attorney would be in touch with him and if he showed up at the studio I would call the cops.

The world outside seemed different after this incident. I was *really* broke instead of nearly broke. I couldn't pay my studio rent, much less my home rent, and what the hell was I supposed to do with all the art samples entrusted to me by the artists, all my files, drawing tables, supplies, and the bills? Facing the hotel manager would be difficult. He was such a nice guy and always talked about the losers who skipped out without paying their bills. I was about to become one of them.

Two nights later at one in the morning I parked my station wagon at a back ramp of the hotel and proceeded to empty out the studio. It took two trips and most of the night, but with help from a friend I got all of it out. About a year later I bumped into the hotel manager, and he told me how disappointed he was when he saw that I had skipped. I felt terrible, told him the whole story that I don't think he believed because he said, "But Jack was such a nice guy."

"Yes he was," I answered. "I thought so, too."

My father—in—law got in touch with Jack's attorney, who was his cousin Jerrold. "We've been through this with Jack before," Jerrold said. "When he was treasurer of his Boy Scout troop he stole all the money they raised, then he did it again in business with another man."

"Why in hell didn't you tell me this when we were putting together the corporation?" I asked.

"The family thought he was better," Jerrold said.

Jack hadn't stolen more than $1,000, but that was a lot of money in the late 1950s. It could have covered the entire year's rent on the studio or paid all our outstanding bills. I wanted to sue him for everything he had, but my attorney just wanted to get the money back that he had stolen. Sol seemed to buy Jerrold's story and was very sympathetic toward Jack. I took the money, continued paying off the bank loan, and began to look for work. I couldn't get enough freelance work to sustain myself and pay off the back debts. My shame at having gone bust made the decision to look for work in Connecticut much easier.

7

On line in Connecticut

I saw an ad in the *Times* by a company called Landers, Frary and Clark, out of New Britain, Connecticut. I applied for and got the job. Maybe another state would change my luck, although it didn't change Dad's when he moved from Maine to New York. Is this a genetic move?

Lew Purly was the tall, slim, white-haired aristocratic manager of the Landers, Frary and Clark art department. He did the New York interviews and hired me on the spot for $100 a week. That was a good salary at the time. The combination of my ability to do layouts as well as illustrations was what he was looking for. I didn't know that this move would time—warp me back to the nineteenth century.

The company building was an old New England factory, all red brick and a block long—right out of a Currier and Ives print. The floors, even in the offices, were wide, rough—hewn planks, more than 140 years old. Huge, vertical bare beams of oak supported vast spaces of these floors, and the building was impossible to heat. We were always cold. I got even colder when my first paycheck came in at a salary of $90 a week instead of

132

the $100 agreed on. My meeting in Lew's office didn't go well. He conveniently couldn't remember offering me more than $90, and I was stuck there. We had no money left for a move and no place to move to.

I was having some clothes altered at the only tailor in town, and I became quite friendly with him. "You know the owners of Landers have their suits altered here don't you?" he asked, and he continued on as though I had answered yes. "Everyone thinks the bosses have only one suit because they wear the same one all the time, but that's not true. They buy four or five suits all the same so the workers won't see them in different ones and tell the workers they can't afford new clothes either." So that's who I was working for.

Exactly two weeks after Enid and I moved to Connecticut, Landers went on strike, and I became "the scab who smoked cigars." The announcement from the bosses stated that we the executives (that's a laugh) either go on the assembly line or they couldn't afford to keep us. I just got there and didn't have enough for carfare to anywhere. Each day as I crossed the picket line the shouts of "there's the scab who smokes cigars" were hurled at me. This was easy—they weren't singling me out because I was Jewish. I had given up cigarettes and was smoking cigarillos. Fame comes in strange ways.

I was put on the assembly line to grind handles for the Coffeematic, electric coffee pot. I ground thousands of handles in the weeks the company was on strike. I made certain that few, if any, were usable. I don't know who cheated me out of my $100 a week salary, but I did know who would pay for it.

Across from me, on the other side of the moving belt that carried finished handles to be assembled, was Danny, a deaf and

133

mute man. We could only use hand signals with one another to convey a thought or greeting. One day he brought in a signing card. It showed me how to hold my fingers and hands to indicate letters and words in sign language, and I was off into another world. This actually made the whole strike worthwhile for me. He knew the word before I had signed two or three letters of it, so it really worked. Danny was a very intelligent young man who had been in the printing department before the strike, and the noise from the presses bothered everyone except him. He expected to stay there the rest of his life. He had a girlfriend and a car and would have liked to get married but couldn't afford to. You don't have to be deaf to be poor, but I'm certain it helped.

John Rolecki, a Social worker I met at the Junior Chamber of Commerce meetings, was complaining to me about his new Catholic wife Jane, who wouldn't let him touch her before they were married but was screwing him to death now. All during their engagement John had complained to me that Jane wouldn't have sex with him. Now, apparently he had more than he had bargained for.

He told me that he could help Danny get a good job that would support a better lifestyle than any of us were used to. "Because of his disability we can get him into a two-year printing school run by the union, which will automatically put him in a good job when he graduates." When I told this news to Danny, he was elated. I set up a meeting between him and John. John worked very hard to put it together, and Danny was ready to enroll for the following year.

Wednesday evening, a few weeks later, I answered a knock on my door and there was Danny with a look on his face that I hadn't seen before. He ranted and raved in semi—mute sounds and waved his arms and signed much too fast for me to understand what was going on. The strange sounds coming out of him were frightening. I calmed him down, and the gist of all this was he would not go to school because he had to leave his car and his girlfriend for two years. I tried to explain that these two years would make the rest of his life very good. His girlfriend could visit him on weekends and bring the car. "*I would go to the school if I could because it means a life of security,*" I told him.

"That's the same thing John said to me. I don't care, I'm not doing it," he signed. *What a fucking waste,* I thought. There was no way I could get through to him.

I saw John that weekend and we commiserated about all the time we had put in to make this possible for Danny. John told me that this is what happens more often than not, and I shouldn't feel bad about it. "You tried," he said, and continued to talk about Jane's sexual appetite. I wondered to myself what would go through Danny's mind about ten years down the road. He missed the only boat that would stop for him, and I hoped the realization wouldn't break him.

My co—workers in the art department were an interesting, if rather odd bunch. Lew sat in his little cubicle and did nothing except stare out the window until we brought him something to critique. There was Arthur, a very talented older art director from New York; one local, ex—high school football jock star, Jonah, who was building his own home on week ends and nights and fell asleep several times each day because he was so tired; Ted Chenden, the writer; and me. Ted didn't work in the same space with us, but wrote the copy for our direct mail and ads. Ted sat in the open factory, near the assembly lines. He was a good writer with a college education a wife and three kids and was paid only sixty five a week. I'm glad I screwed up those handles.

Ted was a preacher's son right from the farm and as sweet and innocent a man as was put on this earth. At six feet four inches tall and skinny as a rail he looked exactly like who he was. He didn't stay that way forever.

"Hey Murry, I spoke with Maud," Ted said, "and she said it was okay to bring you home for lunch, all right?"

"Sure, Ted that would be nice," I said. I hadn't met Ted's family, and this was a chance to make friends with one of my fellow workers. Enid and I, as usual, didn't move into Jewish neighborhoods or join Jewish clubs. We didn't belong to a synagogue either and that didn't sit well with the practicing Jews in the community. Why shouldn't everyone live anywhere they wanted to? Be friends with anyone they want. I never could understand meeting with only people who think like you do and act like you do. What can you learn from them? There is that comfort level of acceptance though, that can't be found anywhere but with your own kind, whatever that means. Is there anything more your own kind than the human race? We all belong to that. Why isn't that enough?

Ted and Maud had three well—behaved kids. As we sat down to lunch I thought I was back in Bangor having my only meal with the McAlisters. Bread and gravy, but no milk for the kids this time. When they asked for milk, Maud said, "Your father didn't bring any home today." Christ, I would have bought milk if I had known. Why did Ted invite me knowing there was nothing to eat? What little there was, was served with pride and could just as well have been a lobster dinner. There was small talk and laughter, and their sense of dignity humbled me. Ted and I became fast friends fighting a common enemy, Landers Frarey and Clark.

Enid and I visited with the Chendens numerous times over the year and a half we lived in Connecticut, and they visited with us as well. Maud told us about her children being born in an *almost* converted chicken coop, the premature stillborn flushed down the toilet, and their struggle out of poverty. They didn't know it, but they were still there. I admired how they handled their struggle with pride, but I did not want to be like them any more than I had wanted to be a junk man like my father. I knew there was better and I was going to get it.

• • •

Fifteen years later I bumped into Ted in a bar in New York City, where he now lived, separated from his family and working at a high—powered ad agency. I was working at a place called Art Staff Studio at the time, and the bar was on the corner of the block. Ted had become an overweight hick turned loose in an alcoholic world of human predators. He thought he had finally made it. I listened to him and saw what he had lost and become.

• • •

When Enid and I lived in New Britain, Ted had introduced me to Frank Casa, an artist he knew. Frank and I also became fast friends with a strong base of mutual interest in art. When he graduated from the University of Iowa, Frank had applied for and received a Guggenheim fellowship and a Fullbright grant, which ran concurrently. He was very talented and a delight to be with. His knowledge of art history and his willingness to share it gave Enid and I many hours of enjoyment.

137

Frank and his wife, Cele, are little in stature but huge in heart. (To this day we stay in touch and visit each other even though we live a considerable distance apart.)

One of the other friends I made was Steve Totten, a local newsman who was always brimming over with the excitement of what he was doing at that moment. At this moment Steve told me he was engaged to a lovely young lady named Marie. He and Marie invited me to be one of the wedding party. Steve had agreed with his future in—laws to marry in a Catholic church. It didn't offend his Protestant upbringing. A couple of days before the wedding I got a call from a very upset Steve. "Murry, I don't know how to say this. The priest says you can't be in the wedding party because you're a Jew. You can be a guest but not in the party. I can't believe this," he said. "I told Marie that the wedding is off if this happens."

I knew the wedding wasn't off and that Steve was just trying to show me how upset he was. "It's okay, Steve," I said. "Just get married and I will be at your wedding. Don't screw up your relationship with Marie and her family before you get started."

"This has *already* screwed it up. After we marry, I'm going to get a job away from these people. I won't bring my kids up to be contaminated with this hatred."

"It's not the family, it's the church," I said. And he knew I was right. Author/historian Karen Armstrong calls it "The Oedipal Christian fear of the parent faith." I call it, "looking over your shoulder and they're still there."

At the wedding dinner Marie's mother made the best lasagna I ever ate. It spoiled me for any lasagna in all my years since. Large noodles in a semi dry sauce with pieces of chicken and sausage and crumbled mozzarella in between the many layers. I wasn't becoming inured to the indignity of being kept out because I'm a Jew, I still remembered the insult—but that lasagna.

• • •

When I left for work at Landers one day, it had been raining for about a week, and the ground wasn't accepting any more water. I got into the car and started driving downtown when a wall of water about three feet high seemed to come out of nowhere. It hit the left side of my car, lifting me and the car up onto a grassy bluff, then it flowed past. I didn't know how lucky I was to get pushed to one side. This became known as the great flood in Connecticut in the summer of 1954. New Britain didn't get hit too badly, but we couldn't drive outside of the town. Enid's sister, Bara, was in a summer camp in the mountains of Connecticut, and Fran called in a panic because the lines were down and they couldn't contact the camp. I packed a lot of food and flashlights and set off to the rescue. I got to the edge of town and the road disappeared into a sea of floating dead cows and large tree limbs. North of us was devastation. It was like looking out at an ocean without the waves. Fortunately Bara's camp was situated on a mountaintop; everyone survived until the water receded and food could be brought in again.

• • •

Ninety bucks a week didn't go far enough, so I sent Enid to Hartford with my art samples. It wasn't easy getting her on the train. She was nervous and unsure of herself, and I literally pushed her up the train steps. Boy was she different when she came back late that afternoon. Hartford Insurance saw my samples and ordered a poster to be designed and illustrated. A female rep was unheard of in Connecticut at that time, and that may have contributed to Enid's selling my work so easily that day. She was about ten feet off the ground, and I felt exonerated about forcing the issue. After that I couldn't keep her home. She wanted to show my samples whenever she could. Freelance work began to build up, and again I allowed myself to be seduced by the lifestyle. I quit Landers and went on my own.

It wasn't as easy as I thought getting freelance jobs. The companies loved my work and gave me plenty of encouragement, but they gave most of their work to established people in the area. I earned barely enough to survive. When I later announced to these same companies that we were leaving for New York, they seemed startled. I told them, "I have to leave to survive, you aren't giving me any work." I wonder who they thought I was working for. There were only so many sources of work, and now the New York studios were sending salesmen up this way to get what little there was. The New York salesmen would wine and dine the art buyers from Connecticut when they came to New York and this was a great attraction for them.

Enid was pregnant with our first child, Lowell. We had no family around, and Enid felt this far more deeply than I did. I hadn't had any family around for so long that it didn't affect me the same way. Coming from a middle—class family without the benefit of having learned from sisters who had kids, was really hard on Enid. She was strong and smart and gutsy, but she had nothing with which to relate this experience and neither did I. New Britain was not on the cutting edge of medicine either, and the mistakes that we allowed in our youth and ignorance were numerous. The doctor insisted on total x-rays of Lowell in the womb in the ninth month, "So I will not be surprised." he said.

The placenta was not fully removed after the birth and Enid passed what looked like a large, dark brown, smooth stone and then we were both scared to death. "You women can't nurse a child, better get bottles," the doctor told us. "Your nipples are not big enough, they're inverted." *You don't come from peasant stock* is what he really meant, but we did come from peasant stock. We were "too civilized," he said. That's where Enid drew the line. She did nurse, though not for long, but she did it successfully against the doctor's wishes and without strong backing from me.

Lowell was born at the New Britain General Hospital on August 28, 1956. Enid's mother came up two weeks before Lowell was born but left before the birth. She couldn't face it. Instead, she sent Louise to stay one week. Louise was the maid who had been in the family for twenty years and raised Enid and her sister, Bara. We put Louise and Lowell in one room, and Enid and I hid in another. For the five days she was with us, we let Louise do as much as she could to lighten our load.

Lowell cried for three months, night and day, as nonstop as anyone can and drove us crazy. We boiled bottles, mixed formula, changed and washed diapers, and slept on our feet. We were not prepared for parenthood, at least not parenthood like this. We couldn't even walk across the floor without him flailing his arms about—any noise at all startled him. The doctors told us it was colic. What Lowell had was an impaired neurological system, which wouldn't be diagnosed correctly for another nineteen years. The widespread medical view in these days was a Freudian interpretation that Tourette was a psychologic, not physically based illness. Psychiatrists and psychologists told us repeatedly that most of Lowell's problems stemmed from a domineering mother and dysfunctional family life. Enid refused to believe this.

For most of those years we took him to doctors who told us we were imagining things. For many of those years Enid knew about and suspected Tourette Syndrome, but would not allow herself to believe it because she feared an old wives' tale that Tourette's comes from a domineering mother was true. It was too much of a reflection on her. I believed there was a connection between the series of X-rays the doctor insisted on and Lowell's Tourette Syndrome.

Neurologists told us we were too demanding. Psychiatrists sent us into years of therapy "for Lowell's sake." They didn't know what was wrong and wouldn't admit it, so they blamed the parents. And the parents were too dumb, too overworked, and too tired to understand what was happening. The Freudian view of Tourette Syndrome had replaced the original, correct, diagnosis of Gille de La Tourette in the 1800s that the disorder had a physical not emotional causation. We knew one thing—we had to keep going. With all these things happening any faltering and our train would go off the track.

Some sixth sense warned me that when Enid cried on my shoulder at night about terrible thoughts of shoving the stroller with Lowell in it, in front of oncoming cars, I had better take it seriously. What Enid had was postpartum depression, but it was not recognized by the doctors in New Britain. Less than a week later our New Britain saga ended. I called Enid's mom and dad and said, "We're coming back to Forest Hills, Enid is not acting right. I don't know what's wrong, but she will be better off there." Within two weeks, we were living upstairs in the second bedroom of my in—laws' house in Forest Hills, with five month old Lowell.

We didn't stay at my in—laws' house for very long, aunt Belle (she didn't like the name 'Bella' anymore) was able to get us an apartment nearby. I got a job as studio manager at Caru Art Studio and earned a steady $175 a week. With this princely income plus overtime and freelance work, we were doing well. We began thinking past our new apartment to a house. Enid wanted out of the Forest Hills apartment.

Enid was pregnant with our third child, Evan. Lil had been born almost three years after Lowell and was a doll—she actually slept at night. The long flight of stairs just inside the front door of our apartment made it very difficult for Enid. We had to move somewhere, but what could I afford within an hour of my job, which was on lower Manhattan right off Maiden Lane? Nothing much. We finally found a house in Bellerose, Queens, one hour and twenty minutes, two subways and one bus transfer from my office. I borrowed $3,000 from my uncle Sam in Maine, and he sent me a check for the amount and an IOU to be filled out and returned. Where it said interest, he put none. I didn't know how generous this was until I borrowed money from my aunt Alfreda when I needed capitol for business and she had me sign a note that paid 10 percent interest. My father—in—law labeled it usury, and it was. We paid it all back. Fran and Sol also loaned us money to go into business and later told us to forget it. What a burden they lifted from my back. What a difference in families.

8

Bellerose, Queens
Five Years in the Wrong Place

It was an all—brick veneer, Cape Cod house with a Bondstone front. The entire property was 60 feet wide by 120 feet deep with a wonderful fenced—in back yard. We stayed there for five years, until Lowell was ten, Lil was seven, and Evan was five.

The neighborhood, unknown to us when we bought the house, was made up of an almost equal split between Catholics and Jews, and the only thing that held them together as a community was taxes and a mutual fear of blacks moving in. Medium—sized maples lined the streets, and children played everywhere—white children, that is. We didn't know what hate and fear we moved into. The struggle to survive and bring up a healthy family apparently wasn't enough of a challenge for these people. Does hate give them a better paycheck? It doesn't, and fear and ignorance really turned them sour.

Six months after Enid and I moved in, we decided to have a party and invited the people we had met on our block. They all accepted until the Jews found out we had invited

Catholics and the Catholics found out that we were Jews. Then they all started calling with excuses, and no one came. And then we knew, too. It wasn't Europe in the Dark Ages, but the distrust was still built in. The difference now is that it's a stand—off.

I met some interesting people on that street, people I could enjoy being with, but they didn't believe that any other way but theirs was the right way. Who the hell was teaching this kind of separatism and elitism in our communities? How would their kids grow up and live in the more integrated world of the future? It took me four more years to find a piece of property of my own, away from people like this. I didn't want to bring up my kids in this environment any longer than I had to.

One evening the doorbell rang and there was a cop and my friend Sadiq. "Do you know this man?" the cop asked.

"Yes, I do, he's a friend of mine. Is there anything wrong officer?" I answered.

The cop turned and left without saying a word, and Sadiq came in. It was his first visit to our new house. "See, Murry, what did I tell you? Just because I drive a Ferarri and am black these guys stop and hassle me. Every time I go to or through a white neighborhood, it's like a warning not to come back. I think the cops are in cahoots with the neighborhood people." I thought he was crazy then. He was crazy like a fox.

Sadiq was doing the same kind of work I did before I started selling for art staff. He was freelancing and working as an art director when he could get a job. I was doing a lot of production work for the J. Walter Thompson advertising agency at this time, and he needed a steady job. I stuck my neck out to try to get him a job there. One of the art directors who had been giving me work was leaving, and although no black art directors

145

existed in this white bastion, he was hired on my say so. What a feat! It was the right time because businesses were being pressured to integrate. Here was someone who came recommended and was known. I really felt good about it. Sadiq was tall and good-looking with a princely bearing and this helped. Another reason for wanting my friend in there was that an art director I didn't know might get the job and cut me out of the work I was already relying on. That would really hurt my commissions on this new job. But that's exactly what Sadiq did to me—he cut me out.

"Sadiq, what's going on, what happened to the work? Isn't any work going through?" I asked.

"Oh sure, Murry."

"What do you mean, where is it , why aren't I doing it?"

"I've been giving it to my brothers, they need the work."

"For Christ's sake, so do I, and I got you the job. What are doing? I told you that the group, head art director let me choose someone for your position so I could continue getting the work that I got before. Did you take the job knowing you were going to cut me out?"

"I'm sorry, but that's the way it is," Sadiq said.

I was stunned. Sure, his black brothers probably did need the work more than I, but loyalty and gratitude surely cross color lines. We ate together, hung out at my place together for years, and talked black and white politics together. We were friends, or so I thought. I would not have given the work to my Jewish friends if the situation were reversed. I should have known when he brought me his 30-30 Winchester to keep for him that he was too angry with whites and too deeply involved in some underground movement. Civil Rights didn't preach collecting

146

guns. After much soul—searching, I contacted his boss, the man whom I had pressed to give him the job in the first place and explained what was happening. In three weeks Sadiq was history. He was not replaced. His work was dispersed among the other art directors in the group some of whom I was already working with.

Many years later I received a call from him like it was the next day. "Murry, this is Sadiq, I'd like to come and get my rifle, when's a good time for you?"

"Sadiq," I said, "I gave that thing away a long time ago. I had no idea where you were and I didn't want it around the house."

He was furious, but there was nothing he could do. His rifle was where I left it, in the woods of Maine with a real woodsman.

I had been on a fall hunting trip with John, the creative director of a famous perfume house. Hunting wasn't really my thing. I make this trip into the woods annually because being in the woods made me happy. Ray Jalbert of the famous Jalbert family of guides met us at the cabin on Round Pond, situated in the Alagash Wilderness of Maine, one of a chain of lakes and ponds the Alagash River flows through. As I understood it, the state of Maine allowed the Jalberts to keep this cabin in perpetuity because their family was one of the first to come down from Canada to settle and tame the wilderness.

The camp at Round Pond consisted of three log cabins. The one for us 'Sports' had a wood stove and slept six in two—tiered bunks. The shack for the guides was narrow and dark with built—in bunks jutting out from one wall. The third was the cook shack with a stove, sink, and table that would seat eight. These cabins sat on a small peninsula of land that reached out into Round Pond, through which the Alagash flowed. The land was as wild as is found anywhere in our country now.

Once, about ten years earlier, I was here with Ray's legendary uncle who was known as The Old Guide. We did some wonderful fishing and canoeing together. At eighty he could still toss me around. The strength of men who live and cut timber in the woods all their lives is extraordinary. We who sit behind desks and eat too much because of the pressures we put on ourselves to build a bigger house, buy a better car, to just plain get more, do not know what men can be. These were men of unusual vigor, strength, and recklessness.

Ray had bagged a deer the night before John and I got there and hung it in a tree so the animals wouldn't get it. He allowed my overeager potential client to put his tag on it so he wouldn't go home empty—handed.

Ray was an enigma. He was a sensitive, hard—drinking thirty—seven—year—old woodsman with an understanding of the politics of the world; a Democrat in a Republican land. He wasn't a large man, just very compact. He didn't move or say more than was necessary. His features were finely chiseled with an unusual thin—lipped sensitivity, and his face was lined with the rivers of Maine. Ray told me that he spent many weekend nights in the local jail to sleep it off, but he didn't drink when he guided Sports, and although I once was a Mainer, I was now a Sport.

I was using Sadiq's 30-30 rifle, John had his fancy 30-08, and Ray was using an old bolt—action 30-08 with a wood stock that was literally splintering.

Charlie, our World War II pilot, had flown in to Round Pond to take us back to Moosehead Lake. I always enjoyed first hearing, then sighting the small plane as it taxied in for a water landing. After our four days of fishing, hunting and roaming through the woods, we boarded the plane for the trip home.

As I climbed the pontoon, I turned and tossed Sadiq's gun to Ray and said, "You deserve a better weapon than that thing you're using Ray. Take this one." The woodsman stood there looking at me and let a tear come to his eye. I felt great about what I had just done. As the plane took off John turned to me and said in a testy manner, "I would have liked that gun if I had known you were giving it away, Murry." One of the things that destroys my calm and makes me rage against humanity is greed like this. A poor man who needs the tools of his trade and, by comparison, the rich one sitting next to me thinks he should have been given the gun. That was my moment to say, *"I will get you a better gun if we can do some real work together, John."* But I couldn't say it. *To hell with his account. To hell with the money I spent to woo the bastard*, I said to myself. Our relationship effectively ended there.

About five years later I met John on the Hudson River line train, headed to points north. We were both going home from the city, me to the Croton—Harmon Station and John further up the line. He seemed a changed man. He told me his wife had left him, and he was trying to understand how a woman could leave a man like him. I could have told him, but he had enough hurt to contend with at that time.

My trips to the Alagash ended abruptly when I got a call from Bob Jalber's son. It was the afternoon before I was to go on another trip up the Alagash. Bob, cousin to Ray and son of the famous old Maine guide, was to take us up the Alagash for his second time. Tall, easygoing, and deferential, you wouldn't have known he was an attorney. He told me about a new, young pilot with a new plane that he wanted to use for the flight from Moosehead Lake into Round Pond, and I couldn't dissuade him. Charlie, the world war two flyer, was the pilot I always flew into the Alagash with in his Beaver. I was superstitious enough to give Bob an argument about the new pilot. But he kept pressing me in our phone planning. I should have insisted.

His son sobbed as he told me his dad had just died taking off with the new pilot. They were on their way to fix up the camp at Round Pond then come get me at Moosehead Lake. The plane stalled at an altitude of about fifty feet above Eagle Lake, where they were taking off, and plunged into water that was no more than thirty—five degrees. A few minutes of consciousness is about all you have at that temperature. They couldn't get to the plane fast enough to save either of them. I remember bruising my hand badly on one trip and sticking it over the side of the canoe into the water. Just like an anesthetic, it was that cold and numbing.

This incident really shook me up. It was the second time a member of the Jalbert family had been killed coming to meet me. Another Jalbert didn't even get as far as Bob did. He was in his truck with his sixteen—year—old nephew, headed for a river landing to pick up the canoes when he crashed. It killed both of them. I received a similar call that time.

I had been up the Alagash River with the Jalbert family ten times in the past twelve years and felt like I was a part of the river and the family, too, but I couldn't do it any more. I couldn't ask another Jalbert to guide me.

• • •

"You mean you don't believe in God? You'll go to hell and burn," said Joey, as I lay in my bed one Saturday morning listening to the kids in the back yard just outside our bedroom window. Joey was talking to Lowell. Joey was one of the Catholic kids from the big family up the street. I don't think Lowell even had a concept of God at that time.

"What do you mean 'burn down there?" asked Lowell. "It's cold down there. It's hot up there," and he pointed toward the sun. I felt very proud of his answer. A humanist, commonsense answer at six years old. Lowell didn't know how very difficult that idea would be to sell in this neighborhood.

Enid had begun what would become a lifelong relationship with the Ethical Culture movement, and I went along. Neither of us felt a great affinity for the dogma of our birth religion, Enid even less than I. We both enjoyed the Jewish holidays, and the teachings of many of them were important to us. It was the blind belief in a God that stopped me in my tracks every time. If it couldn't be explained, I couldn't go along with it. With all the terrible things happening to good people in this world, where the hell is God?

We took Lowell to Sunday school classes at the Ethical Culture Society, in Manhattan and listened to Algernon Black's eloquent sermons. Over the platform, in the auditorium at the society were the words: Wherever Men Meet To Seek The Highest Is Holy Ground. I couldn't argue with that, but that was as far as I was willing to go. Too much had happened in my lifetime to hand over control to anyone else.

• • •

151

My working day, leaving the house for Caru Studio, was from 6 AM to whenever. Mostly whenever and sometimes seven days a week too. I needed all the overtime and freelance work I could get just to pay the bills, much less move us out of there. When I got home, sometimes at one in the morning I might get a few hours sleep. More than likely I would be in our $2.50 rocking chair we bought at the Salvation Army. It was the most comfortable chair for rocking children we ever owned—the arms were situated just right so the weight of the child wouldn't be tiring. I spent hours upstairs in the wood—paneled children's rooms rocking Evan over my shoulder while he twisted with stomach pain from Celiac disease. The doctors explained Celiac's disease as an inability to digest milk products. It seemed to us that the children couldn't digest much of anything. One doctor, whom we called the Banana Doctor, had the kids living on just bananas until we finally went to Columbia Presbyterian and got help from doctors who knew what they were doing. Both Evan and I would fall asleep as we rocked, and this allowed Enid to catch what moments of rest she could. I don't know how Enid stood up to it all day. I spelled her whenever I was home.

Very late some nights, when things were what other families called normal and I wasn't at the studio, under lights in our little back yard, I would execute ink brush drawings on paper. These brush drawings were a welcome change from the commercial work I did all day long. They helped me get through the days and became my signature work in later years. When I had my first gallery showing of these brush drawings in New York City, I didn't take it seriously enough. It was a beautiful gallery, just off Fifth Avenue on 61st Street in spacious rooms filled with light. My uncle Ben from Forest Hills came to see my work and spent some time looking at the ink paintings. Just before he left he took me aside and said, "Murry, please tell me what I'm looking at. What are they supposed to be?" Strangely enough, I admired him for this admission. The only other person I know who would say something like that is me.

I wasn't able to handle praise or criticism about my work, which had become so personal to me. I sloughed off the show and the media by leaving town with Enid that afternoon for a vacation.

•   •   •

"Get your ass back here, I'm quitting," I said. Charlie Halgren, the owner of Caru Studio, was hunting in Africa. I was running the place day and night, and suddenly it was too much for me. My children were becoming strangers, my wife a caretaker of the home and children. I had had enough. I put a phone call through to Nairobi and told Charlie I was quitting unless a better way of working and compensating me was achieved. Charlie came back immediately and made nice to me, all the while hiring his old friend to replace me. I knew what was happening, and it made me sad to think it was so easy for him to let me go. Charlie's brother—in—law, George, was the bookkeeper and receptionist and a really sweet guy. Even he couldn't understand why Charlie wouldn't let me buy in and become a part owner. My attorney was my father—in—law, and I knew he had my best interest at heart. Charlie had no intention of sharing anything except the work. The day I left, George cried each time we talked. I finally found someone more naive than I. Charlie and I went through the motions of getting our attorneys together, but they were just motions.

November 22, 1963, was not only my last day at work but my wedding anniversary as well. I left Caru feeling dejected, went downstairs to the bar under the building and ordered a drink. As I lifted my glass, I saw President Kennedy's head shot off in Dallas. The bartender shouted, "It's about time," and several men from my side of the bar leapt over the counter and started beating on him. Everything in my world was in an uproar. I went into the bar's phone booth, drink in hand, closed the door, and called Enid. We wept together over the phone for all our losses.

Leaving a good job was a trauma to me. I had no idea where my next buck would come from, and seeing President Kennedy killed somehow made it all part of the same picture—no job, no president, no plans, no future.

This was the beginning of a series of assassinations in the United States that marked our lives forever. My family and I watched and wept as Bobby Kennedy was shot in the head by Sirhan Sirhan. Martin Luther King Jr. was next. I didn't take it seriously when he spoke and said, "I may not get to the promised land with you." King's death struck me the hardest, after that of Mahatma Gandhi. These were men of peace. They were all killed on my watch. What went wrong with my generation? Something definitely went wrong. And still, that elusive God.

In 1962, I made arrangements to drive to a particular African American church in New Jersey. On a bright Sunday morning, I walked into the church and sat down in the back. A member came down the isle to find out what I was doing there; my white face stood out. I explained to him that I wanted to be in the march on Washington and had spoken to someone on the phone. "Was it you?" I asked.

"Yes," he replied.

"Are you and your church going on the march? I would like to go with you," I said.

He looked me over as if there was something strange about me and said, "Please come outside with me, please."

I followed him out, around the corner, and into his home where he took a jacket from his closet and suggested I wear it. This was embarrassing. I was in a T-shirt (no holes in this one), trying to make a connection with the history that was about to be made, and he was teaching me how to dress for church. We went back into the church and, after services, I met with the board and the pastor and everyone else and found they were eager to hook up with a white group. They had chartered buses and would be happy to share the space and the costs with us. I also sensed that just as I felt marching would be safer with a black group, they felt they would be safer with a white contingent. We were all nervous.

I brought them together with the Ethical Culture Society of Queens, where Enid and I were members at that time. It was a good combination. After a couple of meetings, arrangements were made. Many of the members of the society went on the same bus with members of the church.

I wanted to take Lowell with me, but Enid was frightened that it would end as a riot and my brother—in—law, the gun maven studying to be an oral surgeon, insisted that if I took Lowell he was coming too, and bringing his rifle to protect us, so I dropped that idea.

Everyone tried to dissuade me from going to the march. I was becoming a little worried myself, but I just had to go. The drive to Washington began with some apprehension, but that soon disappeared as hundreds, then thousands, of other buses and cars joined our caravan. I was moved to write this poem.

A small trickle of a mountain stream
rushed but gently swirled around.
Dipping and turning with each change of the land
at once swelling then being absorbed.
Along the banks past towns and inlets
the stream coursed on
with a weight and purpose
at a rush at a still-over shallow rocky ground,
gaining depth and resonance,
welcoming other streams into its main.
Way deep came the bed
with a roar into the river
and there was a stream no more,
but a vast moving mass
assured of its power
certain of its course.
People waived from the banks
no slowing now
the weight too massive
the turns of the giant down and around
then behold the open way
to the heart of the land.

That afternoon I stood on the steps of the Lincoln Monument, about thirty feet in front of Dr. Martin Luther King Jr., as he gave his famous and moving "I Have a Dream" speech. It was a rare and beautiful moment—the most peaceful and satisfying event I ever attended.

• • •

After I left Caru Studio, I freelanced for a while again, then took a job uptown as a salesman for a studio called Art Staff. The money I made working as Art Director and doing free—lance never seemed to be enough. The family had needs that were getting heavier and maybe a shift within the same field would change things. My starting salary draw was $100 a week against commissions. That was $75 less than I had been making, not counting overtime. The first year I didn't think I would cut it. I owed the owner, Mike, more than I made in commissions. Seeing my resolve weakening, Mike assured me that he would cancel what I owed him if I began to bring in some substantial work. Then something interesting happened. I connected with the J. Walter Thompson Advertising Agency, the biggest such agency in the world at that time. I began to bring work into the studio from the Pan Am art directors and the Ford art directors. At the same time, my persistence was being rewarded with work from some pharmaceutical companies in New Jersey and Manhattan. My financial situation was changing quickly. Mike didn't cancel one red cent.

• • •

We took a week's vacation that summer of 1962 in a small cabin at a camp in Yorktown Heights, New York, called Karger's. Lil, age three was sick the entire time we were there. When we got home we took her to Columbia Presbyterian. The woman doctor there was wonderful. She held out a lollipop and you should have seen Lil's eyes open wide. The banana doctor wouldn't let her have any candy. Lil had never tasted a lollipop.

"She probably has cystic fibrosis," the nurse at Columbia Presbyterian said. Lil had worn a salt patch test on her arm for a week, and the nurse was sending the patch to the lab. "We'll let you know next week. More than likely she has cystic fibrosis," she said again. *Cystic Fibrosis kills*, I thought, she knows that.

"Can't you tell us something now?" we pleaded with the nurse.

"Not until next week," the nurse said cheerfully. There was something sadistic about that bitch. She knows the suffering we'll go through until we hear the results and she has to say, "It probably is cystic fibrosis," not once but twice. "Fuck her. FUCK HER."

The results of the salt test turned out to be celiac disease, as we had hoped. It was by far the lesser of two evils. What a difficult and complicated life it was becoming. After this diagnosis we realized that Lowell had celiac disease, too, but much less severe. Neither of them could have milk products without suffering severe stomach cramps afterward. They would be on formulas and special foods, and still their little digestive systems were not normal. Lil was worse than the boys—her stools were like the white of an egg and her diet was extremely limited. Celiac wouldn't kill you but Cystic surely would.

Even with all this crap in our lives (an appropriate use of words), Enid and I rarely missed a night of loving each other. This, above all else, created a bond that would not break. We were able, for short periods of time, to separate our feelings for each other from sickness and bills while we slipped into the loving, caring mode, so important to our survival as a family.

"Congratulations Murry, Congratulations Murry." What the hell was going on? I had just come back to work from a week's vacation in Canada at the World's Fair with Lowell and with Harry Treleavan and his son, Bruce. Harry was the chief honcho on the Pan Am account at JWT, and that's what precipitated my suggesting the trip to him. He was also divorced and trying to figure out what to do with his son for a week. His son and the fact that he wasn't an easy man to spend time with (and he knew it), prompted him to jump at the offer. Harry didn't talk unless he had something to say about his work. On vacation this meant he had nothing to say. He was pleasant enough, but so ill at ease with people that he projected his unease to all around him. I knew this much about him and found it rather easy not talking with him. Harry was in his fifties, a small man of about five feet seven with the face of a WASP male model and the body of a sedentary executive. As we walked with our sons from shows to rides, very few words were exchanged. Harry was happy and so was I. I have always admired, and appreciated, the fact that Harry would not let me pay for him even though he was an important client. Meeting honorable people from time to time helped balance the greedy ones who proliferated in this business.

Harry and his son decided to cut their vacation short, leave Canada and go back to New York two days earlier than Lowell and me. I didn't know he was directing the Nixon 1962 run for the presidency through J. Walter Thompson. When I got back to New York and Art Staff Studio (I was still working there at the time), there were production mechanicals about Richard Nixon's campaign for president on all the drawing boards. Everyone in the studio was congratulating me. Not saying a word (typical of Treleavan), he made up his mind and without telegraphing his intentions he brought the work to the studio in my name, no strings attached. I didn't realize that history was being made. Haldeman, Ehrlichman, and sometimes John

159

Mitchell were in the large meeting rooms at JWT when I delivered work to Treleavan. I still have correspondence on White House stationary from Dwight Chapin. I started looking for a place to live far away from Bellerose.

About six months after I left Art Staff I bumped into Mike in the Chanin Building barbershop across the street from his studio. We were very civil to each other. The truth is I really liked the man. He had introduced me to this Barber shop when I first came to work for him. The haircut was great but strange things happened there.

It was back when I was still working for him and had just finished getting a haircut there. The barber brushed me off, I tipped the barber, paid my bill, and then couldn't find my coat. A new one hundred dollar coat purchased no more than a week before. The shop owner was incredulous, as if he didn't even know me. He asked all the men to please leave their chairs for a moment and get their coats off the wrack. There was one coat left and he said, "OK, that's yours." I had walked in with a new Hart Schaffner & Marks grey herringbone and what was left was a torn, greasy, old coat that should have been used for rags. He repeated "That's yours." "Look at the suit I'm wearing and the shoes," I said. "Do I look like I would wear something like that? You know me for Chrissakes. I work with Mike at Art staff. Someone swiped my coat and left theirs." He just stared blankly at me. I guess his insurance was on overload. "O.K." I said to him, "let me use your phone. My Insurance agent is right around the corner in the Lincoln building, I want to let him know immediately but I'm not wearing that thing out in public even if it is freezing cold." My Insurance paid for every penny. When I went back to the barbershop after that I always put my coat where I could eyball it.

Early years in the advertising business nearly crushed my pure, almost childlike understanding, of what was right and wrong. Greed pervaded most everyone around me. Many of the people I worked with in advertising were not like Harry. Joe, one of the art directors for Pan Am at JWT insisted on $5 for him in every job. That doesn't sound like much, but I did twenty small jobs a week for him and other studios did more. I tried to dissuade him again and again, but to no avail. I allowed myself to be soiled, at least that's what it felt like to me.

Before Enid and I were married, she had worked in the advertising office at Barricini Candy Company in Long Island City. My first meeting with her boss, Terry the advertising director, was brutal. "I want 20 percent of everything you bill here and in cash. just add it to the bill." Those were almost the first words he said to me. I was so stunned that I had no answer for him, either yes or no. My relationship with Terry didn't last long. He never submitted any bills to management, just stuffed them in his desk drawer. He was holding a politically appointed job and didn't know what the hell he was doing. When all the suppliers started complaining about not being paid, he was fired.

While still working at Art Staff and years after the Barricini account, a man who looked like a bum from the street came up to the nineteenth floor and asked for me by name. He had long dirty hair, rolled—up dungarees, and was emaciated. I didn't recognize him at first, but the voice and mannerisms brought it all back. It was Terry. He acted as if he was still wearing a three—piece suit and just dropped in for a chat. "Listen, Murry, I'm in a rush to catch the train and left my wallet

161

at the office. I need carfare and will return it tomorrow." I handed him a ten without saying a word. I knew there wouldn't be a tomorrow. I knew I wouldn't ever see him again, but what the hell, he was obviously down and out. What happened to his life? Terry was upper—class and well educated. My God, it was easy to fall off the perch.

9

The Difficult, Wonderful Years
of Success and Distress

"Murry, I saw an ad in the *New York Times* today for a house that sounds good," Enid called from the other room. It was Sunday morning, *New York Times* time. The children were out in the yard playing; we weren't taking them to the Ethical Culture Sunday School this morning, so there was time to talk. We had been actively looking for a house for the last two years and had seen almost 200 houses within a fifty-mile radius of the city. Five years of controlled hate between Catholics and Jews and both spewing the same openly for any black family who might look at a home for sale on this block was more than enough. Business at Art Staff was picking up, and this looked like the time to make a move. I called the agent listed in the ad and I drove up to Westchester County that same day, not expecting very much.

It was another world, only one hour from the city just outside of Croton—on—Hudson, New York. The real estate agent drove me up a pretty, gravel country lane called Furnace Dock Road. Two miles the other way at the Hudson River, there was

163

no trace left of the old furnace that used to fire bricks for the area. There were no sidewalks, no streetlights, no house numbers, and very few houses.

Across the street from the house I was interested in, the agent told me, was a home on eleven acres with a marvelous stream rushing hell bent toward the Hudson River. Up the road another family lived on thirty—five acres with three homes and a greenhouse. A short walk down the road and left on Oak Lane there was a small, man—made lake. Three streams that meandered through the low area in back of the Button's House flowed through the small, upper lake then into Lake Woodrock, an old cement dammed and walled lake that held the six beautiful, watery acres. The lake was deeded to about thirty houses on the south side of Furnace Dock. The house I was looking at was one of them. The lake was a jewel, and its future importance to our family was still unknown when we purchased the house. Enid and the children would spend many happy hours on the small beach with neighbors and their children. Other than an annual community picnic, I don't ever remember seeing more than ten people there at one time. There were several homes right on the lake, and an informal homeowner's association managed the maintenance.

The house was set back about 150 feet, nestled into the side of a forested hill on two and a half acres of magnificent land. Very old red and white oaks and maples covered the hill and back acres. The front half acre was lawn with an occasional boulder and 200-year old rock maples along the driveway edge. Tall weeping cherry trees, growing from the plateau banks like mystic guardians, dangled wind—blown limbs above the road. In the center of the lawn there was an oval patch of deep green pachysandra; in the middle of this was the most impressive growth of all—three Hydrangea shrubs had been planted so long ago that they were now trees. I walked under them in amazement, gasping at the huge white blossoms.

To the right, giant Montana Mughos grew from beneath a ledge of smooth, black, rock outcrops. Beyond the pachysandra was a huge gray boulder about ten feet tall and twenty feet wide and long, with trees girding it tightly as if to keep it from rolling away. Two of the trees seemed to be growing on top of the rock. Their roots reached down into the earth and became Evan's ladder. He would use the top of this rock as his first acting stage. He called it his office and collected old pipes, interesting pieces of bleached wood, and bottles to store between the roots. When I went to work in the morning Evan would go to his work atop the boulder. When I was home on some weekends I watched him act and duel with imagined adversaries. Enid and I would double over with laughter and delight and quickly conceal ourselves below the windows of the dining room when he glanced our way. I nailed a railing and a kind of wood platform together to make it easier for him to emote and challenge his mystic world.

The original owners had built the house as a summer cottage, then used the house year—round when they retired. After they died, their children used it summers for a number of years, but tired of it when their own kids got older. It had been rented out for a few summers, then left vacant for years. The house was *almost* livable. I was blinded by the beauty of where it was situated and ignored the poor condition it was in. I wanted it. It would prove to be the best investment of our lives, both financially and emotionally. I called Enid and hearing my enthusiasm she said, "Go for it, Murry." I think she would have said that just to stop the looking. My hand shook as I wrote out the binder check for $500, then I drove back to Queens.

The Bellerose house sold in no time, but my neighbors got a few last licks in. "Murry," said one of the neighbors who dropped over for the first time in the five years I lived there, "I hear you are selling your house. We wouldn't want any difficulties after you leave because of the kind of people you sell your house to. We're not prejudiced, or anything, they just don't fit here."

When black families came to look and liked the house, I would sit them down and say, "I will sell you this house if you want to buy it, but first let me tell you about the people who will be your neighbors." Each one thanked me and never came back again. I could see the distrust and disbelief in some of their faces, and I didn't blame them. Talking with them reminded me of 1962, the year I marched on Washington with half a million black faces.

· · ·

We bought the Furnace Dock house for just over $35,000. This was an enormous sum for us to contemplate borrowing from the bank. We moved into the house in March 1967. Twenty—seven years later, after much alteration and sweat equity, that house had a market value of $300,000.

It was early spring in northern Westchester, and the earth still clung to patches of ice and snow in shaded places. We drove up the driveway past the low granite garden walls on both sides culled long ago from massive boulders of the Croton Dam and waited for the moving van coming from Bellerose with our belongings. Lowell stepped out of the car, looked around at the acres of lawn and rock and trees and asked, "Where's the back

166

yard?" He didn't understand that *all* of this was now our back yard. When we explained it to him, he lifted his arms straight out from the sides of his body, took a deep breath, and as he ran over the property, holding his arms out, a long wailing sound that I can only describe as primal, burst from him. I believe the earth and rocks and trees understood him, as I did. He felt a sense of freedom, a deep intake of breath and life Lowell hadn't yet known and I hadn't experienced since my boyhood fishing in the woods of Maine.

A new way of life was beginning for our family, a life of plenty in a community very different from Bangor, Post Avenue, or Bellerose. A community of privacy, individualism, and history to build on. We would live in this house for more than twenty six years of great changes. We were about to begin the defining and last significant period in our lives of living together. The kid from Bangor who slept in so many basements, as did his grandfather in the basement of the synagogue, was now a squire. "Squire Murry," they called me jokingly, when friends came to visit. I loved it.

This was again a mixed community of Christians and Jews, and we chose our friends not knowing or asking what their religion was. We didn't care. The Jewish community did care and was suspicious of us for all the years we lived there. Most of them didn't go into a synagogue more than two or three times a year either, but they "belonged." They paid their dues and were members.

We went to the Ethical Culture Society in New York City on many Sunday mornings and to some of the Jewish holidays at the Temple in Croton—on—Hudson. My business partner, Ron

Josephs, a devout Catholic, would say to me, "The children have to be something, you can't let them be nothing."

"Isn't a good human being enough?" I answered him.

He couldn't understand me. I found out why he couldn't about nine years later when I wanted to get out of the business and he turned on me. He was a very insecure man, so he needed a name—tag he knew, a tag that immediately placed you in a jar with the correct label on it. I don't buy into this kind of labeling and have paid a very high price over the years for holding that position.

I think Lowell also paid a high price, in reverse. The closest Lowell got to religion through us was the Ethical Culture Sunday school, where he was taught wonderful, ethical values for humans to live by. To Enid's and my surprise he came home after high school one day and announced, "I have become a member of the Croton Temple. I like Rabbi Robinson. His son and I are good friends, and all my other friends belong there." In our desire not to take religious sides we had overlooked the fact that our children had minds of their own and had been taught to use them. Lowell, at age sixteen, was the first to assert his right to choose. Rabbi Robinson took him in as the youngest person ever to be accepted as a member of the Croton synagogue. His desire to follow Jewish traditions and holidays stays with him to this day.

• • •

We started our five-year improvement plans almost as soon as we moved in. Bob Vila would have been impressed. It meant five years of additional bank payments on top of the mortgage, but we could afford it at that time. The kitchen needed quite a facelift, and the floor covering was broken up, too. There was no place for the washer and dryer, and the walls were all cracked. More new flooring was needed in the small room, which used to be the dining room between the kitchen and the magnificent living room. Down three steps was the sunken living room, where wood beams spanned the width of the thirteen-foot high ceilings. At the end of the room, French doors opened into the dining room, which was originally the enclosed, all–glass sun porch. To the left, in the corner of the living room, a massive granite fireplace extended from floor to ceiling and easily accepted four–foot logs. Wood cabinets and intricate radiator covers, stained walnut and darkened with age, were works of art built into the walls by skilled carpenters of the early 1900s. The living room was bathed in light from the thirteen–foot–wide and six–foot–high series of connected iron casement windows.

In 1972 we initiated the next plan of expansion. A staircase from a small room, which was the original dining room, going up to and expanding the attic with a thirty–two–foot dormer. I remember the excitement of pushing a notched two–by–four with five workmen, each with his own pole, to lift the roof and put it on top of the prepared in–place stick wall.

For the next twelve years Enid and I had our master bedroom, bath, and a second small bedroom upstairs. We found a carved newel post at an outdoor junk shop and used it for the addition to connect the old with the new at the top of the staircase. We paid off the 1972 expansion in five years. When the kids had all gone off to college, we moved back downstairs and built a fancy tiled bathroom by expanding the smaller original one. We installed a double, navy blue, whirlpool, cherry cabinets, and a corner shower. We spruced up and took over Lil's old bedroom. This gave us a master suite on the main floor. Even a poor kid from Maine can learn to live really well.

• • •

As Lowell grew older, his behavior, become increasingly difficult to understand. Strange body movements, facial tics, and grunts were a constant source of irritation to us. In our ignorance—and the ignorance of the countless medical doctors and psychiatrists we took him to over a period of sixteen years— we did not understand him as he was. Whatever it was, we felt it could somehow be cured if we could just find out what the hell it was. Teachers at school complained of Lowell's erratic behavior and his inability to finish timed exams. When he got to high school, this problem was seriously getting in his way. Doctors told us we were pressing him too much. School principals fought with us. They were all of one mind—it was the parents' fault. Enid and I went through what seemed to be endless years of counseling, with and without Lowell, but his symptoms persisted, as did our feelings of guilt constantly fueled by the doctors words, "There's nothing wrong with your son. *You* need therapy."

Lil was into animals, particularly horses. There was a barn near us, so we bought our first horse for Lil to keep and ride there. I was elected president of the barn because I was the oldest and lived in the biggest house. I didn't know one damn thing about a horse. Tommy Tinsley, the only black person at the barn, and a monster of a man carrying at least three hundred pounds of flesh, befriended Lil. Seeing them walking together, they made a strange couple indeed.

Many Sunday mornings Lil and I would drive to horse ranches nearby and have a great father—daughter breakfast and

170

watch the cowboys ride. We had four horses, at different times of course. When one would get the best of Lil, we would sell it and get another that she would ride until she spoiled that one too by not showing it who was in charge. I remember Angel the best because she was the last. She was pure white with blue eyes and was just great to watch when Lil rode her. Lil got knocked off by a tree branch while riding Angel, and after that she never really got back into horse riding. She would just lead Angel around, walking in front of her. By the time we sold Angel, Lil was finishing high school, and that was the last of the horse barn for us.

"I'm never coming back to your house again," Lil said. "When I finish with college I will get a job and move into my own place." She was an angry girl who openly rejected our middle class values. She had been something of a recluse through high school. No boys hanging around only horse people and, at times, it was difficult to tell what gender they were. Loose baggy overalls, heavy work boots covered in manure—they certainly all smelled alike. Enid and I tried not to take her sullenness personally and each time she threatened to leave I offered, as I did with the boys, to make them sandwiches. This would either bust her up laughing or make her mad as hell. I took my chances.

Lil seemed to like a little college in Maine. I had the feeling that it was because I grew up in Maine and had talked with fondness to her about my time fishing and walking through the woods there. Nasson College used to be an all—girls school and had recently converted to coed. It was small, in a tiny town with a pleasant campus filled with old dorms. Lil was attracted to it immediately.

We delivered her to Nasson College, spent a day shopping in the little town of Sanford for all the clothes, notebooks, and bric—a—brac she might need for the semester. Enid and I had decided that Lil must work for her spending money after that first semester. We gave her enough money for the semester and told her to get a job if she wanted money for the rest of the year. It might sound kind of harsh when I say it now, but as good as our income was we were still pressed for cash. During Lil's four years at school, Lowell was a student at the School of Visual Arts and Evan was accepted at Juilliard. The boys' schools had no campuses. Neither of the boys could find much work, and their school projects were not limited to the normal hours of a liberal education college. Lowell did photographic assignments all weekend and printed them at night. Demands at Juilliard were just as difficult for Evan. Lil felt that the boys were getting more money and attention than she was, and she was probably right. That was the situation, not the intent. The ride home to Peekskill from the schools in New York City was a good hour and a half each way. When would the boys do their assignments? I had to rent an apartment in New York for them so they didn't have to come home each night.

I was very proud of Lil when I saw how she managed at school. She started out scrubbing pots in the mess hall kitchen and wound up in charge of the kitchen. With her new second—year position as dorm mom came a free phone and a larger room. These things helped take some of the load off Enid and me. I hope Lil knew that. I told her but wasn't certain how much got through. She still "wasn't ever coming back to this house again." I stopped offering to make sandwiches.

I won't dwell on Lil's booze consumption and partying in college. In a letter from her, dated April 18, 1978, she wrote, "It's D Day and all the classes are cancelled. Now the festivities begin, the coffee house opens up and serves Bloody Mary's, Screwdrivers and Tequila Sunrises—FREE!" I assumed the other parents were going through the same trauma.

By the end of her first year, Lil was doing poorly in school, and we got warning notices. We sat her down and laid it out like it was. Stop the partying and bring your grades up to a credible level, or we will take you out of school and you will go to work. We said the magic words, *take you out of school*. Lil loved the school and the environment. Within a couple of months she pulled her grades up to well beyond just passing, and the next year made dean's list. That's my girl.

"Hey Dad, I'm going with this really nice guy I met up here at school," Lil told me over the phone. She had never mentioned a guy before, and something in her voice got my attention. "He's a year ahead of me and will graduate the end of this semester," she said. I waited for more but nothing was forthcoming.

"So," I said.

"So," she said. "We may move in together when I graduate next year."

I knew there was a *so*. There would be a lot more *so*'s shortly.

Lil was preparing to come home after graduation next year. "Come home to this house?" I heard myself saying into the phone. I stifled my laughter, but my feelings got through. Lil saw the comedy in it all and took it well. I wanted her to reverse what she said four years earlier and tell me she wanted to come home to my house. What I got was, "Oh, Daaaad."

Evan was into being somebody. Somebody who was *somebody*. He took himself very seriously from an early age and demanded that we all do the same. He bordered on brilliant, but it still wasn't easy taking such a little guy so seriously. Enid and I didn't know how conscious Evan was of the torture Lowell's Tourette was inflicting on us and how he tried to counter much of it by being particularly good and causing no trouble. Years later I realized how sensitive Evan had been as a child and how profoundly he was affected by happenings in the family that the other two children apparently shrugged off.

After Evan wanted to be a fireman, he tried Little League baseball, then drums and a pick—up band, and finally acting. He found his calling there. He was a good actor, and with his photographic memory it brought him very early local recognition, which is what he wanted. Evan knew he wanted to be an actor, and he switched to special courses in high school that helped him in that direction. He graduated before he turned seventeen, was on off—Broadway stages in his seventeenth year and on Broadway in leading roles in his later teens. He seemed to be the ideal contented child, "who had his own." Enid's childhood friend, Bobby Kalfin, whom Enid hadn't seen or spoken to in years, was a well—known director of off—Broadway theater. Evan seemed determined to be on stage, so Enid decided to call Bobby. They met for lunch in the city and talked for a while about the many years that had passed since their childhood together, but mostly about Evan's desire to be an actor. "Sure, have him call me for an appointment," said Bobby.

"But don't expect any special treatment. If he has talent I will try to use him."

Evan went to work as a gofer for Bobby Kalfin's Chelsea Theater group, sweeping up the stage between acts and generally doing whatever was required. They began using him as a script reader with other actors, and in what seemed to me a very short time he was given a small part in *Biography, A Game,* by Max Frisch.

On a plane coming back from a California business trip I was reading *The New Yorker* magazine and behold—five miles above the earth traveling at 600 miles an hour, bursting with pride, and with no one to tell my discovery to—I read Judith Oliver's review of the play, in which she mentions a fine young actor, Evan Handler.

After that he was given a part in Kalfin's play *Strider.* Then the calls from agents started coming in. Evan managed to elude them for almost two years while attending school. Carnegie Mellon University had offered him a four—year scholarship with perks. Juilliard offered to let him in. We tried to convince Evan how practical it would be to take the scholarship offered by Carnegie Mellon. "Ev, we have three of you going to private schools at the same time. This will be very difficult for us. Carnegie Mellon is a first rate school, too," Enid and I said, trying to convince him.

"You don't go through Pittsburgh to get to Broadway," Evan said. He chose the Juilliard School for Acting at Lincoln Center in New York City. Two years later he was offered the part of Lt. Eddie West in the movie *Taps.* Juilliard did not allow its acting students to take professional work while going to school, and this was more than he could walk away from. He left

Juilliard and took the part, certain that stardom wasn't far off. By the time Evan was twenty—three years old, we came to accept his success in movies and on Broadway as the norm. That same year, 1984, in a January 26 letter, he wrote: "The fun that the life affords is the very poison which makes me incapable to do the job" and "I wonder if I'll get to be rich, not famous. Better, I think, than famous, rich, eh?"

10

Success in My Working Life

During the years at Somanydoors (Evan won the house-naming contest) Enid graduated from Queens College then took her master's at Columbia. She became the administrative director for Phelps Memorial Hospital Mental Health Clinic in Tarrytown, New York, with a staff of sixty reporting to her. She worked there for thirteen years, until Evan became ill in 1985. We had both become high—powered, hard—driving, successful people.

Working long hours with heavy responsibility was exhausting, and I needed to do other things for diversion. Besides my ink brush drawings, I had been writing poetry during the 1960s when the civil rights movement was laden with so much emotion. I published 100 copies of my own small book of poetry with the title *Potpourri*. There was an additional fifty insides of the book that were printed without covers. Twenty years later I learned to make bindings for books, and I covered those fifty inside pages in handmade birch bark cloth from a Native American tribe in Arizona and drew a different ink brush figure on the cover of each one.

When the kids one by one reached age sixteen and passed their driving tests, we bought two used cars for the three of them to fight over. With our two, that made four cars in the driveway. Moving them around in a heavy snowstorm was difficult. Many winter mornings I shoveled from 3 a.m. to 5:am, showered , dressed, and headed for the train station.

Ploughing through two—foot snowdrifts at 5:20 a.m. to catch the 5:40 train out of the Croton Harmon Station to New York was a challenge. It's a good thing I bought that secondhand, 122S Volvo. It ploughed through everything but finally died in a snow bank one winter. I think its heart went.

Before Croton built a new train station it was little more than a shack with a bunch of cold people huddling together for warmth in the winter until the train arrived. Coming home at night I would sometimes forget that the ninth step going up the exit staircase was a trap. That step was a good inch higher than the rest and when I forgot to remember I tripped and fell, unless the person in front of me tripped first. My shins were beginning to look like a washboard. If you wanted to know if someone lived in Croton Harmon just look at their shins.

• • •

Those early years of freelance were difficult but sweet. Sweet because Enid and I were terribly in love and having things was secondary to having each other. Difficult because I began to wonder if I would ever earn a good living. My dream of earning $200 a week in my lifetime was fading. I thought that was the ultimate. As we struggled, Enid's family began to wonder if I could ever make a go of this art thing. "But what do you do for a *living*?" I remember my future mother—in—law asking me when

I told her I was an artist. Now I was married and still not making a living, and things were getting hairy.

One of the many evenings we had dinner at Sol and Fran's house, Enid's Uncle Bernie and Aunt Evelyn were there. Bernie had a good job working as a site finder and construction engineer for Waldbaum's grocery chain, but he was also trying to make money on the side selling pizza ovens. Suddenly, as if by happenstance but obviously planned, I was being convinced to sell pizza ovens. What the hell did I know about selling pizza ovens? I was an artist for Chrissakes! A starving artist to be sure, and with no light at the end of the tunnel. Saying no to making money selling ovens, while saying yes to remaining a starving artist put me in a terrible mood. When Enid and I were alone later that night, I ranted and raved about being put in this position while she sat in a chair and cried at her own complicity, her love for me, and our inability to pay our bills.

• • •

I left my job at Art Staff around 1970, I took my clients and went into business for myself. Murry Handler Design Ltd. was the name. Most of my work was production of ads for the J. Walter Thompson Advertising Agency. My attorney, my father-in-law, Sol, felt that "Ltd." was fancier sounding than "Inc." The boss at Art Staff felt that I betrayed him by leaving, and he made parting somewhat difficult. I understood his going to my contacts to woo some of them away. He almost succeeded because the ones who were on the take were afraid he would somehow implicate them. He never threatened to. He couldn't without implicating himself as well. I opened my second office, Murry Handler Ltd. on the corner of Vanderbilt and 42nd Street.

Pick up and delivery of jobs from my new office was all done via Grand Central Station and a few underground walkways. I always kept a pocket full of quarters to give to the pan handlers as I crisscrossed the station and never came up for air. I even went home via Grand Central. In the winter it was great. New York City was heating my route. Unfortunately, much of the work was a call at 4 p.m. to be completed by the next morning at 9 a.m.. That meant working most of the night. If the call came on Friday, it meant working all weekend. This was the norm.

The Hudson line train I took to get home was on the lower level of Grand Central Station, just across from a Fanny Farmer candy shop I couldn't resist. A pound of chunky chocolates to eat on the train, then a full meal at dinner (lunch was usually a full meal and cocktails) with a bottle of wine. This was good living, this good living eventually caught up with me.

I had been seeing clients all day and trying to design all night when I was in my offices on Vanderbilt. I couldn't keep that up. I needed help and unless someone owned a piece of a business they wouldn't put in the time necessary for success. I took a deep breath and another partner. Ron was a good designer and a very serious worker. His people skills were sorely lacking, though, and I did a lot of role—playing that first year to help him understand relationships within the organization. His modus operandi was to verbally brutalize people working under him. He was now a boss and didn't know how to handle it. We moved out of our offices on 42nd and Vanderbilt and signed a lease for the penthouse 630 2nd Avenue at the corner of 40th Street and began developing a staff of fourteen people.

I heard Ron screaming at someone and found him in with our part—time bookkeeper, who was sitting there reduced to tears. Ron said that she very likely had padded one or two hours onto her time sheet each week. I took him aside and explained to him that now he was the boss and yes, he will be ripped off by some people working for him if they get the chance. "You are no longer one of them," I told him and alluded to what he probably did with his time sheet when he was working for his last boss. He began to understand. At the end of the first year together, we were both happy with our decision to form the partnership. We were making money and making a place for ourselves in the New York advertising community.

I 'beat' the New York and New Jersey bushes for design work and creative advertising. Within one year we were working with the largest pharmaceutical companies in the country. It didn't come easily. No one at these companies knew me. The product managers who gave out the work didn't want to be bothered by seeing someone new. When I called from the lobby and tried to see them they would say, "Sorry, but it will be at least an hour or two or three." I sat in some lobbies all day calling up to the managers, every hour on the hour. Eventually one saw me. That's all I needed. My samples and I did the rest. After working with one manager I could easily get appointments with the others.

Each year around Christmas, my family would have dinner at my partner's home, and at Thanksgiving we were host to their family. We never went out socially as a group that I recall. We lived different lives in different worlds. Ron was a religious Catholic, and I a non—practicing Jew. Not reconcilable, but at least we could afford to eat the same kind of food. We did have one thing in common besides business. He had great kids, too, and was even tougher on them than I was on mine. One of his daughters confided in me tearfully, "My dad doesn't trust us." "I know how that feels," I empathized." He doesn't trust me either. I don't think he trusts anyone."

I am not certain when Ron and I started to drift apart and actually feel uncomfortable with each other, but, for her own reasons, our office manager and bookkeeper, Shirley, was putting more effort into driving a wedge between us than doing her job. In the end, between my weariness and her connivance, she was successful.

After nine years together I decided that it was time for me to leave the business. The stress of work and the in fighting with my partner was too much. Our early legal buyout agreement was challenged by Ron and his lawyer. In 1982, after nine difficult but prosperous years, with great bitterness from my partner and a lot of ingratitude from Shirley, I sold my half of the business to an outsider because Ron wouldn't honor our agreement. I understood both of them very well. Even though I had opened a whole new world of earning and lifestyle to him, Ron was petrified that he could not run the business. He wanted me to stay, and no amount of my reassuring him that I would make myself available would change his mind—and since I wouldn't stay, he would screw me over. He was smart enough to run the business and knew enough, he just had no guts. Fear won out.

Shirley, who was heading toward fifty and beginning to worry about her old age, was just plain greedy. They got together behind my back, with the man I was selling my half of the business to and undermined me.

I knew I had to go. I was totally burned out from years of tension, boozing with clients, and stuffing my face with too much of the wrong foods. The high life was over. I took much less than the business was worth just to get it in cash and over two years, not five. My attorney also negotiated one year of restricted access to the clients instead of the usual five. Ron, my partner and friend for nine years, sat mute as his new *almost* partner raged and lied to the attorneys as we tried to settle our buyout. I didn't know then that the new partner had talked Ron into lending him part of the money to buy me out. I doubt that Ron ever got his money back. In the end, they undermined each other.

Shirley was promised a tiny percentage of the business for turning on me. When she reminded them of this, the new partner fired her and Ron didn't open his mouth. This was very typical of him. I had warned Shirley that this would happen. Less than five years later they went belly—up. Fear and greed— what a wasteful and losing combination that was.

The shock of losing my working identity took about six months to get over. Trying to find new clients at this stage meant bucking a lot of young, eager kids who would work at half my price. Setting up a studio in my home was fun, and it occupied a good deal of that first year. Our house was nestled into a hillside with three sides of the basement above ground. With the under— the—house garage eliminated, my working space with a private bathroom was about 1,200 square feet of open area. I built a cutting/storage table using four by eight foot plywood panels, attached a free—form desk to one end that went off at an angle. I purchased a copy machine, a fax machine, and two computers, and hooked Enid up to one Mac upstairs in her office via a floor vent so she could access the printer. I bought one laser printer and then had to figure out how to use all this stuff. No one I knew had a computer setup except the local print and type shop. It was another year before I could do anything billable with my Mac. The Mac came with two megs of hard drive and was upgradeable to four. Pagemaker was the only application I could use then, but it launched a lifelong interest and awe of computers.

Enid was still working at Phelps Hospital and getting a good salary by this time. With the first buyout payment in my pocket, Enid's salary, and a little freelance work, we got through that year. After that, I was no longer obligated to stay away from my former clients and friends. Pfizer began giving me work again, and so did American Cyanamid. I wasn't a company anymore, so my workload had to be limited to what I could do by myself and a freelance helper. It was great getting back to the drawing board after chasing clients for so many years.

11

Lowell

We were certainly not overprotective parents. Not protective enough as I think of it now. We sent Lowell to a National Wildlife Federation Camp in Paducah, Kentucky that we never visited. At 13 he took a plane, waited hours in airports and stayed for a month at an outdoor hiking and camping oriented camp. Apparently when he told them he was a Jew they were so shocked that he became an oddity to protect rather than hurt.

Lowell took another camp trip with an outfit called Trails West a few years later. This one we thoroughly investigated. According to Lowell the counselors started all the kids on pot and sex, even though some of them weren't old enough for either. Several weeks after he came home from a cross—country road and hiking trip with them we found hash balls in his room. At first I didn't know what I was looking at. Enid and I discussed it and finally realized what it was. He flushed them down the toilet and promised never to do it again. Boy were we naive. This started Lowel on the road to self—medication and what I would call an addiction to pot. Evan was more subtle in his use. I never

185

heard Lil talk about it. All the kids around were using marijuana as my generation had used beer and booze.

"Dad, you're always knocking the stuff and you never even tried it. Why not give it a try just once. OK, I thought to myself, maybe this will give me some insight to the kids and then I can say something with authority and they will listen. We sat on our front deck, Evan, Lowell and I and passed a joint around. I had quit smoking long ago and it was difficult inhaling and holding it in as I was instructed. The boys got giddy and a little silly and I got nothing out of it. "I don't know what you kids see in this stuff? It tastes awfull and besides being a waste of time, it's illegal." As I spoke to them from my now vast experience, I found myself looking down from above, at the three of us talking and smoking. What the hell was happening? I was petrified and couldn't get back down to my body. The fear was intense and with my body suspended it seemed to last forever. Moments later when I told the kids what had happened to me they said "great, cool" and stuff like that. "That was a terrible experience," I told them. "If that's supposed to be fun you have weird needs. It scared the hell out of me." I never tried pot again.

Enid and I still couldn't find out what was wrong with Lowell. None of the doctors we took him to had a name for his convulsions, grunts and body jerks. In his frustration Lowell kicked holes in the walls of his room, smashed glasses, and generally allowed himself to go out of control in his demands on Evan and Lil. No doctor or shrink seemed to know either. We fought with teachers and principals over his behavior and his inability to cope with many normal day—to—day routines. Enid pressured the high school principal into giving Lowell untimed tests, and his scores finally went up to where they should have been.

How do you explain to a teacher that just because Lowell is jumping in the air and kicking himself in the butt doesn't mean he isn't like everyone else? How do you explain that just because his arms shoot out from his body in jerky motions, while he barks like a dog that he isn't doing it on purpose? We didn't know his behavior had a name. . . Tourette Syndrome.

"Thank God for the camera," became a mantra I repeated to myself again and again each day. Lowell bought a 35-mm camera with the money he received on his thirteenth birthday (Lowell called the gathering of the Ethical Culture Clan his mock mitzvah instead of his Bar Mitzvah), and it consumed him. We built a small darkroom downstairs in the basement, before it became my studio, and photography became his passion. We soon learned just how talented he was. Somehow, even with his jerky motions and jumping, he held still when he clicked that camera. He took pictures of everything wherever he went—and he was good. He had a different eye than most, a different perspective to shoot from. In the first competition he entered at 16 he won first prize. An esteemed psychyatrist from Westchester County came in second.

The camera didn't take away all his frustrations. He had great difficulty reading because the words appeared to float off the pages or invert one line over the other. Lowell was obsessive-compulsive as well. Everything had to be repeated or said over and over again until it satisfied some inner scale in him. This was all part of the syndrome, as we later found out. It caused him great distress, and he took it out in ways that were damaging to our home, his well being, and, unknown to us at the time, his two younger siblings as well.

After a difficult ten—hour day at work, I came home to find he had again, out of rage and frustration, shattered the repaired walls of his room by kicking in the plaster walls right down to the studs. I lost it. I took the tripod—which he prized second only to his camera—went out to the front deck and smashed it into a twisted piece of steel against the granite wall. Then I told him, "If you ever trash this house again, your camera will get the same treatment." He never did it again.

The one thing that kept Lowell and us sane was his people skills. He had more friends than anyone I had ever known. They really loved him and simply took his strange actions in stride.

In some ways he certainly did act like most other kids his age. One night, I came home, late as usual, and as my car lights flashed past the glass sliding doors of my ground floor studio I saw an unclothed woman's shape race across toward the bathroom.

When my children were in junior high school, I set a very strict code of behavior in our home. No messing around with anyone, no drinking, and no drugs. I expected them to live up to this code under my roof and hopefully everywhere else. At times I would come home to the three of them parading in front of the house with signs saying "Welcome Warden." This time, Lowell broke Murry's law.

As I entered the sliding doors to my studio, Lowell was sitting on the couch in the cold without a shirt and sweating profusely. It didn't take a rocket scientist to realize what was going on. I wondered how he got his pants on so fast. My studio was below ground on one side; in the winter, without a fire in the wood stove, it was uncomfortably cold. As his sweat dried and he began to tremble, I kept my overcoat on and sat and talked small talk with him for about thirty minutes. I knew the naked body in the bathroom was suffering, too.

It was a quickly arrived at way to handle the situation, and although it didn't deter him forever, he remembers it to this day. At that time I'm certain he knew that I knew what was going on. As I went upstairs there was wheel screeching as her car shot out of the driveway. I didn't mention the situation again until Lowell was a grown man and we could both laugh about it.

"Mom and Dad, I have to leave school and this house and get myself cured," Lowell said. "I know I can do it, but it must be on my own." At nineteen, Lowell was leaving home. After two difficult years at The School of Visual Arts he was quitting. None of us knew the cause any more than he did for his weird actions, so we let him go. Enid and I gave him our Saab with a two—way radio and $500 and kissed him goodbye. We didn't know what else to do with him. John Longo, our neighbor and friend, rushed into our driveway, hugged Lowell, and gave him a $20 bill. I remember the mixture of feelings watching the Saab pull out of the driveway. I had taught him how to drive in that car. He learned faster and was more coordinated than either Lil or Evan and he twitched and grunted the whole time.

I felt relief that he was going, guilt that I felt relief, and fear for his safety. I left my father's house when I was seventeen, but that was going into the navy, a controlled environment. *At nineteen he should be able to survive,* I told myself. And then he was gone.

189

About a month went by before we heard from Lowell. When he ran out of the $520 he left with, Lowell stopped in New Orleans and washed dishes at a restaurant called Trios for just enough money to flop in a motel right across the street for the first night. Once he got acclimated to New Orleans and in and out of a number of jobs, he settled down and spent the better part of the next two years living in a marvelous apartment in the old section of town and looking for a cure for whatever it was he had. Trios gave him a permanent job waiting on tables, but it didn't last very long. Lowell's compulsive motions and need to touch people combined with his body jerks and deep grunts, was just too much. The customers needed a quiet place to eat, and that wouldn't happen with Lowell around. The owner taught him how to cook. He made friends at Trios and, as is usual for Lowell, they remained friends for a lifetime. It was in New Orleans that Lowell would first hear the words *Tourette Syndrome*. Nancy, a nurse friend of his he met while volunteering at The Greenhouse, a short term home for runaway children, suggested he might have this neurological problem. Lowell called the local hospital, but couldn't find anyone who knew what it was or had even heard of it. Surviving the moment was uppermost, so he temporarily stopped his search.

New Orleans was special for Lowell. Several excerpts from his letter of June 7, 1997, to us showed clearly how he felt. "There are people here who are helping me, people that I came to with an open heart, and they gave me the same. . . .This is an area which is almost unimaginably rich in its diversity of cultures. . . . It is important that I photograph here simply because there are people here."

Two years later, a wiser, older Lowell came home and returned to the School of Visual Arts for his bachelor's degree. We still didn't know for sure what was wrong with him. Much later, Lowell went to the New School to earn his master's degree, and then taught as an adjunct professor at both schools.

When Lowell finished school and was doing freelance photography, we invited a couple of his older well—known friends—he had friends everywhere and at every level—to a fancy dinner at Somanydoors. Lou Myers, the famous cartoonist who drew the poster for the original *La Cage Aux Folles* Broadway production and the bi—centennial cover of the *New Yorker Magazine*, and Leonard Freed, an internationally renowned photographer, also came. These two hadn't met previously but knew *of* each other. It was a splendid meal. A ten pound standing rib roast (not affordable now), plenty of good wine from the cellar, and what I expected would be great conversation. I hadn't taken into consideration the two strong egos and how they would interact. When I glanced over at them, they were deep in discussion.

Suddenly, my head jerked up from my own conversation with Bernice, Lou's wife, a wonderful artist in her own right.

"Fuck you, you don't know what the hell you're talking about," Lou was shouting.

"Fuck you, too," Leonard shouted back. "Don't tell me I don't know what I'm talking about."

"I'm going to punch you out," Lou said, pushing his chair back against the wall and standing up with his hands in an old—time boxing position. Lou had to have been at least sixty at the time. I knew him as a brilliant man with a very short temper.

This was the first time we had met Leonard, who was at least fifteen years younger than Lou. Putting together an old Bolshevik with a young capitalist may not have been too smart. The wine didn't dull their senses, it just made them more confrontational. Lowell jumped up and calmed them down. He walked Lou into the living room for a while, and when Lou came back he concentrated on the food and wine. By the end of the evening, Lou and Leonard were friends again, and I believe their friendship continued to their deaths.

Things were calmer when we invited Oliver Sachs, the brilliant author of such books as *The Man Who Mistook His Wife for a Hat* and *Awakenings*, to our home for the weekend. Lowell had just come back from his travels with Oliver around Europe, England, and the United States. They were becoming fast friends, and Enid and I were eager to meet him.

"Mr. Handler," Oliver's voice came over, the phone in his car, the third time in as many hours. "Maybe we better call this weekend off. I can't seem to get there even with the directions you gave me." Lowell told me later that he was notorious for getting lost in his car.

"Tell me where you are," I asked.

"I'm at a Texaco gas station on route 202. That's all I know," he said.

"Great, I know exactly where that is and I will be there in less than ten minutes."

"No, I don't want to impose," he said in his clipped British accent, "let's just do it another time."

"This is no imposition. We are very pleased to meet a friend of Lowell's. Please wait, I will be right there."

"If you insist," Oliver answered.

The weekend turned out to be wonderfully interesting, full of Oliver's and Lowell's stories about their trip together. Oliver really relaxed that weekend and late at night, as he played Chopin on the baby grand Enid inherited from her mother, the music floated through a very contented and proud household.

• • •

"Dad did you hear that?" said Lil. "He is talking about Lowell." It was Dick Cavett on TV describing what he said was a "new" disease called Tourette Syndrome. The description was exactly Lowell. Armed with a name for his bizarre behavior, the psychiatrists suddenly got smart and said, "Yes, it is Tourette" and "Would you bring him in, please? We would like to examine him again. We've never seen anyone with Tourette."

"Oh yes you assholes have. You just didn't know what you were looking at and you aren't getting a second chance at him." Lowell was twenty—four years old.

• • •

In a letter from Lil at school, dated September 29—after we had received an official diagnosis of Lowell's Tourette, she wrote, "I was upset to hear about Lowell but then I got to thinking that it's good that he's finally being helped. And now he can lead an even more normal life than he already has been. I've been thinking about the kind of person Lowell is. For someone who has what I consider to be a major handicap all of his life, he's a normal person. I don't know if we realize just how screwed up he could have been if he wasn't the strong individual he is and if he didn't have parents like you two. Actually we've got a lot to be thankful for once we accept the fact that Lowell has a disorder."

12

Happy Birthday

Enid and I received a phone call from Evan the night of Thursday, September 18, 1985, asking that we meet him and his girlfriend Jackie, at the Mt. Sinai Hospital in Manhattan. "I think something is wrong with me," Evan said. "My blood test results will be available, and I would like you there."

This kind of statement, though unusual, didn't set off a total panic. I told Enid, "Hell, it's probably nothing. You know Evan. He always thinks he has something bad."

Enid and I arrived at Beth Israel Hospital Friday morning and went up to the hematology unit on the fourth floor. As we stepped out of the elevator, I glanced to my right and saw Evan and Jackie, in the hallway leading to the doctor's private office, holding hands and sitting on the floor leaning against the wall.

"The doctor just took a bone marrow sample from my hip," Evan offered, "and we're waiting for the results."

"How did you know anything was wrong?" Enid asked him.

"I went to my doctor because my throat was sore, and I am feeling so tired all the time," Evan said, his hand still holding tightly to Jackie's hand. "The doctor noticed some red spots in the back of my throat and asked me if they were anywhere else. I showed him how there were some on my ankles and stomach, too, like little stars. He told me they were called petechiae. He took a biopsy from the back of my throat and sent me here yesterday to deliver it personally to Dr. Nixon. We were told to come back for the results today. That's why I called you. After seeing the results, he needed to look at my bone marrow, so he screwed this thing that looked like a wine corkscrew into my hip and extracted some marrow. That hurt. My white blood count is extremely high, and he wants to be certain of his diagnosis. I think I have something bad," he said all in one breath. That was a profound understatement.

We waited for more than five hours in that antiseptic hallway, until the doctor had finished with all his patients and until other doctors examined and confirmed Evan's bone marrow sample. A feeling of foreboding settled over us. I held Enid's hand and rubbed her back as much for my own sense of security as consolation for her.

When the doctor finally came out, he asked us, in a quiet somber tone, to please come in. He scurried around, trying to move books and papers from chairs to make some space for all of us, insisting that we sit. Evan sat on the edge of a chair directly in front of and almost touching the doctor's desk and steadily rubbed the left side of his cheek, as the doctor recited his mantra of death.

"I am very sorry to tell you that you have acute myologenous leukemia. Of this I am certain. Other doctors have

195

viewed the slides and concur. That is why I kept you waiting so long. This is something that must be addressed immediately. The hospitals are having some successes and" — his voice turned into a monotone sound that wouldn't stop"— and your white cell counts are dangerously high"—and the hum of his voice continued. Evan kept rubbing his face harder now. There was absolutely no other movement. No one else uttered a word. I lost all sense of time and understanding of what was happening to us in that cluttered, dusty room with no life, no air, no intelligible words—only sounds of death. " If it were my own son"— the doctor said, and the hum continued.

Evan's voice suddenly jarred me back from where I had gone. "Okay, let's get out of here," he said. We all stood up as if by command. This was the Evan we were to see much more of in the hospital years to come, the Evan who took charge of his treatment and saved himself.

The doctor's words of apology and regret followed us as we filed out of the office, down in the elevator, and out of the building onto the street corner. My mind played tricks with thoughts. *I wonder if he feels bad enough not to send us a bill? Is God watching this and letting it happen? Why is it such a beautiful day? Is God mocking us?*

For the first time since this momentous unreal charade began, Evan looked at me on the sidewalk in front of the hospital and I saw the pleading in his eyes. "Dad what do we do?" he asked. We bent toward each other, our heads met, and with no words, just a gesture of my shoulders, he knew that I couldn't do a damn thing this time.

It was afternoon now, and we took a cab directly to Evan's apartment where the unreal real, continued. We talked and wept through useless words, movements, and terrifying visions.

Enid took action. She phoned her brother in law Arne, the oral surgeon, and asked him to call friends who might be connected with Sloane—Kettering so we could get Evan in quickly. It must have worked, because we got a call about eight o'clock from a Dr. Zweig, who was already assigned to us. Evan, who was crying and moaning, pulled it together enough to talk to the doctor.

"We only admit emergencies on weekends, Mr. Handler," Dr. Zweig said.

"But doctor, isn't acute leukemia an emergency?" Evan asked. "My platelet blood counts are very low."

"Maybe for other hospitals, but not for Sloane—Kettering," the doctor replied. "Take my home telephone number, call if an emergency arises, and if you start bleeding you can come in. No, you don't have to call, just go to the door on the east end of the hospital; otherwise, see you on Monday." Then he hung up.

Start bleeding? What bleeding, from where? Evan still held the phone in his hand when he burst into a crying and screaming jag that enveloped us for hours. He was screaming and crying in Jackie's arms. Enid and I were in a semi—catatonic state, still not able to fully comprehend what had just happened to our family.

Evan was so upset at this point I felt he needed a tranquilizer, but I didn't know if it was safe to give him one. I decided to accept the doctor's offer and called him back to ask if Evan could take a Valium. The doctor, after berating me angrily told me, "You are abusing the privilege I gave you by calling me."

That finished me off. I put down the phone and felt myself filling with rage, at the same time shriveling inside with shame that I had allowed him to treat me that way because he was the medical savior. No one could know the depth of my pain that night, as we lay awake on the floor listening to Evan cry and Jackie vainly try to console him.

The profound shock of seeing my child in this situation rendered me quite helpless. Until that moment I hadn't fully realized how important each member of my family was to me. They were just always there, always in their place. My thoughts went back to Evan's childhood. Tossing a baseball on the front lawn; exploring along the banks of the Hudson in a canoe, watching him play drums in the school band. He was so proud when he showed me his report card—it was almost always all A's. I forgot to pick him up after a Cub Scout meeting once, and I remember him, a slightly built seven—year—old, at dusk in front of the school with his hands on his hips and tears in his eyes, alone and waiting for me.

That unforgettable canoe and bush pilot trip into the Alagash wilderness where I saw a vision of my dad through Evan. Evan was in the other canoe with one of the Jalbert family guides, and he hooked a huge lake trout. As he struggled to bring the fish in, all of us from both canoes were shouting instructions at him, and he seemed to shrink down inside the many layers of clothing under his parka. The guide reached over the side and hooked his fingers under the fish's gills, and Evan fell back, exhausted, not from the physical effort but from emotion. My father's face flashed in front of me with the same look as when he had hit the drunk who was bothering Mom. Dad's own violence hurt him more than he hurt the drunk. Evan's violence against the fish hurt him the same way.

I yearned for the times of his childhood to be here again when I could protect him and control would be in my hands. I wouldn't allow sickness to touch my son. How proud we were as parents to see the success he had made of himself as a young adult. This kid had it all, we thought. We never contemplated a devastating illness.

· · ·

Neither Enid nor I were able to rally ourselves. Thank goodness Jackie stepped into the void. By the time we got control of ourselves, Evan had been through his initial round of chemotherapy, and we had been shunted to one side to take on a second—string support role. We brought food to his hospital room that he requested but then couldn't eat. We scoured the town for the kind of pajamas that were comfortable for him because he sweat—soaked about seven pairs a night from the medications and fever. We called people and family from around the country to come in, give blood, and be tested to see if they were a match for a possible bone marrow transplant. Product managers who were my clients at Pfizer got on their computers to find me information about leukemia. They had done this for me before with Lowell when he was finally diagnosed with Tourette syndrome. This time we were calling hospitals and doctors around the world to find out how to save Evan's life.

When the Babylonians overran Jerusalem in 586 the Judahites believed that Jahweh had forsaken them. Those exiled to Babylonia didn't understand that they could still pray to God even if it wasn't from a temple in Jerusalem. Their world had come to an end. Some began to lift their hands to heaven in search of their God. I found myself unconciously doing the same thing, standing on street corners in a crowd of people, looking up, raising my hands to a God who was a stranger to me and wondering why. The only correct answer was, *why not?* Why *not* us? We weren't any better than anyone else. It felt like a lottery I didn't sign up for.

The question that kept coming up in my mind was, *if God does everything, He must also do the evil as well as the good. Is this some kind of game for Him? Why didn't Hitler get a disease?* I don't believe a god, any god would do something like this.

When Evan called us, in the middle of the night, frightened that he was dying, we raced to his side from wherever we were. I particularly remember one night when a blizzard was raging over New York. We got a call from Evan's hospital bed about ten p.m. He was totally out of control with fear. How we got to the city from Peekskill, I still don't know. The car slid all over the road, and visibility was zero. At least there were no other fools on the road. When we got to the hospital, the nurses on his floor were very angry that we put ourselves in that kind of danger and delivered a long lecture about losing the parents of patients. Evan was not particularly happy to see us. I believe he was actually ashamed of his fright and of calling us. Then, as his fear subsided, we were pushed away again. At that time, nothing we could do for him was enough or even the right thing. He was determined to survive at any cost; as far as he was concerned we didn't have the right equipment for his survival.

Before this illness, like any child, Evan believed that we, as his parents, could solve just about everything. It must have been a terribly rude awakening for him to realize that we were not omnipotent just when he really needed us to be. In his struggle for survival he began to see Enid and me, and the entire family, as part of his illness. Because of this new view, festering wounds from his childhood, of which we were unaware, surfaced.

"We are not the family I thought we were," Evan told us, as if we had been lying to him all the time. "We are not the perfect family," he said.

"I never thought we were the perfect family," I said.

"How can the perfect family have one child with Tourette Syndrome and another with leukemia and continue to act as if they are okay?" Evan questioned. I didn't know Evan had perceived us as a perfect family. Lil and Lowell certainly didn't.

This became his rallying cry for family reform. Evan felt that these old wounds contributed to his illness by sapping strength from him at this time. By wounds I mean events and relationships between Evan and his siblings and other family dynamics that affected him deeply. Many, I felt, were taken out of context by a child unable to categorize them. Many were the response of an extraordinarily sensitive child, and some were just plain true.

Enid called Evan's attitude "the tyranny of the ill." It certainly felt like tyranny. How could I answer an accusation from a son who may be dying? What sins must I admit to lift this burden from him? What Evan was asking for was release from the responsibility he had assumed as a child. A responsibility whose results, he felt, might have put him in this place. A responsibility no one knew he had taken on. But we should have.

To realize at this late date that I might have missed the boat in rearing the only family I would ever have was crushing. My absence from the home, my avoidance of problems, Lowell's long—undiagnosed Tourette Syndrome and his demand for all our attention during those early years plus my own inadequate upbringing, had finally come home to roost.

"I don't care how he treats us, let's do whatever is necessary and whatever he will allow us to do to help him," I said, and Enid agreed. We decided that all else, including my work and hers, would stop. Our energies would be directed toward helping save Evan's life. "We will not lose him," I said to Enid, not at all certain of my own words.

I had recently sold my advertising design business in Manhattan and was developing a thriving freelance graphic design company working from the house. Enid, seeing my success working at home, said, "I can do that, too," and left her position of thirteen years at the hospital to start a consulting career. The very week she resigned, Evan had called with the news of his illness.

Some weeks later I crashed my car, and Evan was furious with me. He understood what his illness was doing to us, but he blamed the crash on my carelessness and what he perceived as excessive drinking. My drinking was probably excessive during this time, but that did not play a role in the accident. I was in a rush, as always. My own life was on hold; two of my children were sick. Evan was in extreme pain with unexplained high fevers. Results from a liver biopsy were due that day. As I was driving around a curve on an ice—slicked Furnace Dock Road heading toward Route 202, I lost control. The car moved silently sideways, sliding off between two cement pylons as if by design.

In what seemed to be slow motion, the car nosed down over a four—foot stone—wall and came to rest rear end up. During the instant of slow motion I thought of the way a favorite author of mine, Albert Camus, died—a sudden car crash on a rain slick road and bam, it was all over for him at thirty five, then immortality through his writing. Unlike Camus, I had nothing to be remembered by except my children, and I was in danger of losing one of them.

I got out of the car through a back door that was still functioning, walked to a phone about a half mile away. The cops came, my car was towed to the shop, and that was it. It wasn't my time. My attitude suggested that, as Camus was inquisitive to find out how death felt, I didn't much care either way. I was more depressed than I realized and was functioning irrationally. I started being very careful of what I did and how I did it. I had a wife and two other kids still counting on me.

Enid had her own near—death car experience driving west on 287, a six-lane speedway. Her head slumped against her windshield, and she fell asleep. "A pill to relax you," is what the psychiatrist who was working with the family said. It was really a potent sleeping pill. Enid took one at the late meeting she was attending in White Plains, then started home. A man driving in the next car, seeing her begin to veer left into the divider, realized what was happening and leaned on his horn. It woke Enid up, and she regained control as he continued to honk until she took an exit still a half hour from home.

After a number of experiences like this, Enid and I realized we had to be much closer to the hospital. We called everyone we knew to find a place to live near the hospital. Evan had good insurance coverage, but the $1,050 extra a week for a private room plus the same amount for a hotel room and food for us, and others coming to be tested was prohibitive. We were going through money like it was water, and no money was coming in. In spite of all this anguish, some decisions about the future had to be discussed and made. We had two other children whose lives had also been turned upside down by this catastrophe. I made a decision to survive this ordeal for the good of the family. I put aside a portion of myself in a place where I would not allow Evan's illness to invade, a place that would survive whatever the end result of the illness was. The rest of me slowly began to die.

I called Shelley Grossness, a friend I had met through a wine—tasting group Enid and I belonged to. He lived in New York City, and I thought he might know of a place we could stay. Shelley said, "Murry why don't you call the Moraces? They are in the wine club and have a place in New York as well as a place in New Jersey. They are lovely people and if anyone will help they will."

"But Shelley, I just met them a couple of times, we really don't know them."

"What have you got to lose?" He was right and we were desperate.

I called and spoke with Rosemary Morace, told her the whole story, and she said "Murry, let me talk to John, and I will call you back." Well that was a nice way to get rid of me. She was pleasant, but I didn't blame her for politely excusing herself from the situation. I probably would have done the same thing.

The next night Rosemary called, and as she spoke and offered me the apartment, a vision floated round me. There were John and Rosemary passing by with wings and halos and I was standing, looking up at them, tears streaming down my face, down my body, and pooling on the ground, giving me a reflection of my own jaded self.

John and Rosemary Morace (and for the most part their son, Phil) moved out of their sumptuous apartment, which was only four blocks from the hospital. We were given keys, passes, and told the place was ours. No one ever did anything like this for us before. I saw what true kindness and generosity there can be in people. Not a week of my life goes by that I don't remember that kindness.

Between the first and second rounds of chemotherapy, the doctors allowed us to take Evan to the apartment. I thought his getting out for a while would be great, but it wasn't. Walking around in masks, no touching, scrubbing with liquid iodine, and alcohol rubbed on all surfaces. This wasn't really friendly, and the masks did not allow for any recognition of mood or facial expression. Evan wanted to get out of the hospital as a symbol that he had already beaten the leukemia with the first round of chemotherapy.

"If he gets a fever, bring him back fast." Those were the instructions from the doctor. Evan was very unhappy and very weak, his life had been stopped at the beginning of an astonishingly successful career. No matter what we tried to do for him, it was a losing battle. I resigned myself to doing what I felt he was asking for, filling his demands as well as I could and surviving the feeling that I just wasn't cutting it. I still haven't forgiven myself for not being able to somehow miraculously cure him.

The fever came back before a week was out and at 2 a.m. we rushed him back to the hospital for massive doses of antibiotics. This amount of medicine would produce a condition the nurses called 'shake and bake'. A high fever followed by violent chills and shakes that continued, alternating for hours. Evan went through this many times. We didn't know then that it would be five years before we would awaken from this nightmare.

It doesn't take long for the clergy in a hospital to sniff out the really sick patients, and they began paying attention to Evan almost immediately. A young rabbi would come and visit and talk with him. He knew the occupant of that room was Jewish because his door card was coded with a J. He also knew that Evan's chances for survival were not good and that might make him more receptive. Shit, if you think you're going to die and there might be a chance for survival, why not? Anyone from any religious affiliation with a guarantee of life would have been welcomed by all of us.

Evan is like me when it comes to religion and faith. It isn't a part of my everyday life as it was when I was a child praying in the synagogue with my grandfather. It's just something a lot of people do. But I didn't want it. I had faith in myself and what I could bring to a situation using plain common sense. Most important, I had no fear of God (not yet anyway). Evan hadn't been through the basic religious rituals that I had. I went to Hebrew school and did the whole service at my bar mitzvah, but I had neglected educating my children in the heritage of their ancestors. I blamed my father for neglecting to fully explain our faith to me when I needed the strength of knowledge to protect me from the criticisms, taunts, and false assumptions of the Christians around me, and then I did the same thing my father did.

Now, all day and night on every street corner at every restaurant, elevator, doorway, and wall to lean against, I prayed silently to God, anybody's God, anywhere, to save my son. The doctors had given up hope, and I needed a miracle. I didn't believe in miracles. Okay then, I personally wouldn't let him die. As long as I was with him and didn't let him out of my sight, he couldn't die. I'll be my own god, dammit.

While Evan was ill in the New York Hospital and Enid and I were still at Somanydoors full time, I would eat most days at Jeremia's my favorite tavern for lunch and a Rob Roy. My grief would give way to crying quietly and the waitresses, who knew me and knew the situation, patted me on the back as they passed my seat delivering food to the other customers. I found places like this where people accepted my grief and didn't ask questions. It was strangely comforting to me. Nothing slowed my appetite. Jeremias made the best hamburger on the East coast and their tuna salad sandwich on a hard roll came in a close second.

The Friday Enid and I drove into New York City to hear Evan's diagnosis was September 19, 1985, My fifty—sixth birthday.

13

The Wedding

"Dad, Tom and I want to get married," Lil said. I knew it was coming but had several other things on my mind, which seemed to take priority over Lil's announcement. Enid and I realized that this could help get us out of the doldrums Evan's illness had us in. What a great reason to celebrate! Evan was out of chemo and in remission. If he got through the next two years he would have beaten it. It's time to celebrate and really whoop it up, and a wedding was the perfect vehicle. *Evan can be at his sister's wedding. Another milestone. Let's celebrate now! We don't know what's coming*, I thought.

Lil began to fill us in on Tom's family. Both his mom and dad were alive and well. They were practicing Catholics, and his brother was a priest. A priest in my own family fascinated me. It was almost like infiltrating enemy lines.

Tom seemed like a nice guy. The kids were in love, and I didn't want to spoil anything as pure as that. Young love doesn't come along very often. We did the obligatory stuff, like going to his mom's house for dinner. His family came to our house, etc. But during the plans for the wedding I began to feel some discomfort. Memories of my early years of prejudice kept forcing themselves into the present. The Koch family came from the same area on the Poland—Russia border as my grandparents did. Tom's mother, Wanda, cooked food that tasted the same and evoked memories of my bobeh. It felt almost like my own family, except they didn't live in the ghetto. They lived poor but free as Christians, in a land where my people were despised because they were Jews. I know it wasn't their fault that Pope Urban ll summoned the knights of Europe to take part in the first Crusade in November of one thousand ninety five. This Crusade, considered an act of their love of God, tore through the Rhine Valley in one thousand ninety six where they slaughtered the Jews in their villages because (they believed) they were the people who killed Christ. How can Christians hate Jews when Christ was born and died a Jew? This is something my mind cannot resolve. It had become too painful for Christianity to look over their shoulder and see the Jews, who hadn't accepted Jesus as the Messiah, still alive and practicing the Original faith.

How can one massacre in the name of a God? That's either blasphemy or God is bad.

Tom didn't know about my history and I mustn't spoil this happy time. I must turn my mind around as the times have turned and be, if you will, a good Christian and forgive. As the Original, I can do that. We had a wedding to put on, and we were going to do it right.

Lil wore Enid's wedding gown. Enid had saved her gown all these years just for this occasion. It had been wrapped in acid—free paper in an acid-free box and was somewhere in the attic. We were delighted to find it in beautiful condition and even more delighted to find that Lil wanted to be married in it. It fit Lil, except in the chest. Lil was built like my mother.

We had to find a priest and a rabbi to cooperate in the ceremony. It was easy to find the priest—Tom's brother, Gene. He was really nice. When the rabbi was late for the wedding ceremony, he came over and consoled me. "Don't worry Mr. Handler (he stayed formal), I know some Hebrew prayers and will say them for you if the rabbi doesn't show up." I never forgot that. I thought his sensitivity was wonderful. English would have been okay.

Finding a rabbi to perform on the Sabbath proved much more difficult. They didn't like doing this, and the more they disliked it the more money they charged. Tom's was a working family who found it difficult celebrating on a Sunday night then getting up for work the next morning. We acquiesced. A rabbi whom we didn't even know came up from the city and charged $300 for the ceremony.

The wedding was in a small Greek Revival building and former Catholic Church in Cold Spring right on the Hudson River. It was a beautiful little place in a beautiful spot and was acceptable to us and Tom's family. I'm certain they would have much preferred a church wedding. For us, that was out of the question. I don't know what the dynamics within Tom's family were, but my assumption was that he had something of a battle on his hands.

About three hours before the ceremony Lowell, Enid, and I went over to inspect the place and check that no side, Catholic or Jew, would be offended by what was there. Someone had put up crucifixes around the walls and a sash with a large cross on it over the lectern. It wasn't there two days before. I guess the people renting it out assumed it was a Christian wedding and were being helpful. We hid the items in seats and cubbies and left the place feeling pretty good about it. When the ceremony started, Gene came out on the altar with a full—length, scarlet high mass robe and the biggest crosses in gold I had ever seen. I couldn't help smiling to myself. Upstaged again.

The ceremony was uneventful. except for the fact that as I handed Lil to Tom, Tom kissed me instead of Lil, he was that out of it. When the rabbi, in the robin's—egg—blue sports jacket, came forward to do his particular thing, all of the Jews' cameras flashed. When the priest stepped forward for his turn, the Jews sat down and all the Catholics snapped their pictures. Woody Alan could have done something great with this.

The reception was at Plumbush Restaurant in Cold Spring. A large restored estate with Acres of beautiful grounds for strolling and intimate dining areas for romantics. I remember most of the happenings with total clarity, although I did drink enough to loosen my tongue. I remember saying to one of the nuns who came with Brother Gene, "You're too pretty to be a nun."

"No, I'm not," she snapped back at me. Obviously she was right. It was a damn foolish thing to say.

When I picked up my stepmother, Sadye, at a hotel near the Plumbush Restaurant the night of the reception, she didn't answer my buzz, so I called the manager who let me into her room. *Shit*, I thought, would she choose this moment to die and steal the show? Sadye wasn't in the room. I got worried (she had to be eighty, at least). We looked around the front lobby and in front of the parking area. Still no Sadye. I couldn't wait around any longer, so I got in my car and started to pull out of the hotel

211

lot. A small, white-haired figure half hidden in the hollow of a vertical beam that supported the large overhang in front of the motel caught my eye. I got out of the car, went slowly toward the figure, and called out, "Sadye?"

"Who are you?" a voice came back at me.

"It's Murry, Sadye, come on we'll be late for the party."

"You're not Murry," she said. "You don't look like Murry."

Oh shit do I have to go through this now? I thought. "Sadye it *is* me, please let's go."

She moved out of the shadows and said, "You got old, very old."

"Yes I got old, now, please let's go."

"Do I look different? Did I get old, too?" she said. Ten years ago she looked like Methuselah. "No Sadye, you look the same," I said, and she reluctantly got in the car.

• • •

Before Dad died Sadye's life with him had become difficult again. He was pretty much over his angina pain and was out of bed enjoying life for the first time in years. But now his mind was going. Sadye would come home from work and find him totally disoriented. He began to mess himself and not understand what was happening. She hired a woman to stay with him during the day, but she called me and said that she couldn't afford to keep the woman and couldn't stay home because she had to work. I didn't have a spare sou with three kids a wife and a new home in Westchester. Any contribution would have put me in the poor house. I also remembered Dad telling me that Sadye had numerous investments and income. The whole scene didn't feel comfortable. This had not been a marriage made in heaven. It was a marriage of convenience between a lonesome man and a woman who wanted a family she could call her own. Neither of them got what they wanted.

Sadye and I decided to put Dad in a nursing home very near their apartment in Forest Hills so she could visit him often. This would allow her to continue working. Sadye said she couldn't bring herself to take dad to the home, but she called and made the arrangements and Lowell and I did the dirty work.

I pulled the car up to the entrance of the nursing home and helped Dad into one of the many waiting wheel chairs lined up just like carts at the supermarket. With Lowell hanging tightly to my right arm, I wheeled Dad in. It seems that this jolted him back to reality for a few moments, and he looked up at me and said, "I won't eat much, please take me home." Overcome with a swell of emotion and unable to see clearly through blurred eyes, I glanced down at Lowell and saw tears streaming down his cheeks. "Don't leave me here, I'll die here," dad spoke again.

My God I can't do this, I thought. Certainly not with my son here to witness what I thought would be a quiet transfer of a person whose mind had already left him. What am I teaching him? My turn will certainly come someday and I hope I earn more compassion than I seemed to be showing my own father. "C'mon Lowell," I said as we did a 180 and headed for the door. "We can't leave Grandpa here, can we?" I asked him. Lowell just shook his head from side to side, hanging onto my arm, not saying a word. This was only a respite. A couple of months later I did put him in the home, by myself, and he was totally out of it. He didn't even recognize me anymore, thank God.

Less than two weeks later, Sid quit the job she had told me she needed. I don't blame her for not wanting to become a nursemaid. As I said, it was not a marriage made in heaven, but I had been duped. She didn't need to work. She should have been straight with me. In spite of this, I included her in the wedding. I sat her at a table with all my uncles and aunts, not on the dais. I couldn't allow her that honor. Something inside me hardened up I didn't like the woman. I Liked her even less when I put together all the happenings that made up her character for me. She never forgave me for sitting her there. It cost the kids an inheritance.

Dad only lasted a couple of months. He went downhill fast. I took the opportunity to bring the children to see their grandpa, peaceful in his fetal position. "Children, Grandpa is dying. See how peaceful he is? He has no pain and he is very comfortable," I said.

"He's so skinny," Lil said.

"He certainly is skinny, feel his knee," I said as I felt his leg and knee. I did it in a very upbeat way, and the kids got into it with a slight hesitation but no fear. They all felt grandpa's knee and leg, and we straightened his blanket.

Lowell said, "Does he know we're here?"

"I think he knows in his own way," I said. "Not like we would, but he senses us here." I stroked his head with my hand, then leaned down and kissed him. Each of the children kissed him good—bye, too. A few days later I got a call that my father was dead.

We hadn't been close, my dad and me, but the feeling of loss was definitely there. Relief that his suffering was over was there, too. The man who taught me there was no god, that belief

214

in religion was nonsense and that only bad people use condoms was dead. I hope I leave more to my kids.

• • •

"Dad, I have a new girlfriend," Lowell said, as we spoke on the phone. "You know her. She dated my friend Danny when we were in high school. Remember that little blond kid, Susanna? She just called me out of the blue, and we have been seeing each other. She's an attorney now and works in a law firm in Boston. We've been going back and forth to see each other."

Wow, I thought. There wasn't much left to ask after that enthusiastic information pack. "How long have you been seeing each other?" I asked.

"About four months," Lowell answered.

Lowell was now living in Cold Spring, a small town north of Peekskill. Evan kept the apartment on 6th Street and 2nd Avenue for himself. We moved Lowell out because his Tourette seemed to be getting worse, and he had developed a new twitch—he beat the floor with his foot like Thumper the rabbit. The old lady who lived below them was complaining by banging on the ceiling with a broom handle and screaming for him to stop, she didn't speak English so she yelled "benja, benja as she banged, but he couldn't. Living anywhere else, the same problem would arise.

I had just received the last payment from the sale of my half of the design business. Enid and I decided to look into buying a rental building and putting Lowell in on the first floor. No one would hear his stomping. He would be safe there and could act as our representative to the tenants at the same time.

We found a remodeled 165—year—old, five—family house on Main Street in Cold Spring. We gave Lowell a terrific first-floor apartment for very little rent. It made his life easier. He had at last earned his degree from SVA and was working.

Cold Spring was a typical New England small town. This was the town that made the chain that stretched across the Hudson that kept the British from getting to West Point during the War for Independence. You could see West Point from the towns landing looking southwest across the river, which was at its narrowest and deepest here opposite Storm King Mountain. It was a beautiful town and turned out to be a good place for Lowell to live with dignity. This is where he and Susanna had been meeting.

Enid and I knew that Lowell's relationship sounded serious, but marriage wasn't even in our wildest thoughts. He was doing a little bit of freelance photography, but nothing that would support him. We had been through a number of his dashed love affairs, and assumed this was just another one. We were wrong.

Many of you reading this must be wondering what kind of women Lowell could attract with the movements and noises that he almost continuously made. Plenty of pretty ones. Women loved Lowell. They were also very much more accepting of this syndrome than men. They just got past it. This was a bright light in an otherwise socially unacceptable, cosmetic disease. (It also helped that Lowell was handsome.)

Lowell and Susanna fell deeply in love. Theirs was the best wedding I had ever been to and continues to hold that place even though Enid and I had made a beautiful wedding for Lil and Tom.

216

Susanna earned a handsome salary as an attorney and saw no reason to wait to get married. She would help Lowell until he got on his feet. Her parents were another story. Her father had been shell—shocked in World War II, and that interfered with family relationships. Her mother had a less than intimate relationship with Susanna and her sister. Enid was fast becoming Susanna's confidante. After they were married and Susanna moved to Cold Spring, she would stop at our house at least once a week and spend time quietly talking with Enid. Susanna was wary of me because I felt, of her relationship with her dad. We never had a direct, heart—to—heart talk.

14

Baltimore

Evan had been out of the hospital and in remission for two years. During those two years Enid and I went to bed each night after a solemn prayer at having seen Evan get through another day. He wasn't the same boy we had known. He was an unhappy, angry young man with the Sword of Damocles hanging over his head. He did not see us as the same parents whom he knew as a child. He stayed away from us. We still couldn't please him, but I didn't care. He was alive.

But almost to the day, two years later, while in the lead role of Neil Simon in the play *Broadway Bound* on the Broadway stage, Evan relapsed and the leukemia returned. He felt betrayed by circumstances and life.

Enid, I, Jackie, and Evan spent the next year back at Sloan—Kettering trying to get him into remission again. This was a lot tougher than the first time around. There was no quick fix here. For a while it seemed there might not be any fix at all. Chemotherapy again to kill the cancer, unless it killed you first; dozens and dozens of blood transfusions that took hours from Evan's life that he might not have to give; fungus and yeast

218

infections; and enormous amounts of antibiotics, which brought back fevers and the 'shake and bake'.

During this period, the relationship between Evan and I was at its lowest point. We did not talk to each other unless it was necessary. One particular day, I was standing next to his bed giving what feeble, verbal encouragement I was allowed to. Evan looked up at me and quietly said, "Dad I don't know if I can keep this up. I'm so tired." It caught me by surprise.

"Don't say that. I won't let you say that. You must keep fighting. You can't give up." I heard myself shouting at him, commanding him not to die. When I look back at this I realize that the right thing to have done would have been to tell him that it was okay to die. But I couldn't do it. I could only yell at him, as my father had yelled at me when he didn't know what to do. And I didn't know what to do.

No one in the family had bone marrow that was a match for Evan — so he would have an autologous transplant, which meant using his own chemically cleansed bone marrow as the donor marrow. There was no other avenue open to us.

Johns Hopkins Hospital in Baltimore had performed a couple hundred of these autologous transplants, and the survival rate was thirty five percent. This was *not* a comforting figure. But the only other option was doing nothing, and that was certain death. We were taking our last shot.

Sloane Kettering told us they had a fifty percent survival rate with Autologus Transplants. Evan pressed them for the number performed and the answer was "two". My God what a flip, obvious play for more bodies.

We sat in Evan's hospital room in John Hopkins in Baltimore as he pounded the bed and cursed at where he was.

The decision to once again destroy his bone marrow had been made. Evan swallowed chemo pills this time—no more injections of the orange chemical into his veins. These pills would destroy any chance at life if the infusion of his own marrow, which had been removed from his hips earlier and now cleansed of cancer cells did not migrate when they were returned to his bloodstream. Even if they did take, if there was even one live cancer cell that wasn't killed, it would be over.

I tried to imagine the journey of these cells. From his veins, they knew how to get through his bones and begin making new marrow. Miracles were happening, and we couldn't see them for what they were. Our fear and Evan's pain blotted out everything else. Evan knew the torture and uncertainty he was about to endure and was inconsolable. Jackie sat at the foot of his bed with her hand on his lower leg as he swallowed the pills. At that moment, and for the first time in this ordeal, I didn't see any way out that was good. I was really scared.

Four days later, with his marrow almost totally destroyed by the poison pills and no chance of survival without the rescue dose, as his purged marrow was called, it was reintroduced into Evan's veins.

Jackie, for all her courage in other areas, couldn't tolerate this procedure and the awful stink of garlic that it brought with it. She left the room. Enid and I sat across the room from Evan's bed, trying to say soothing things—any things—as we watched the nurse in what seemed to be a slow-motion film. She would carry each large tube filled with Evan's life into the room one at a time and hand it carefully to the doctor, who ever so slowly infused it into Evan's chest, one at a time until all seven vials were empty. The procedure took three hours. The weeks to come would be absolutely heinous, more so than we could have imagined.

We needed to set up properly in Baltimore to support Evan and survive ourselves. Whenever we had to move or do something different or find out about new things, we broadcast it to our support network. When the Gheens, friends of ours from upstate New York, heard we were going to Baltimore, they called someone, who knew someone named Rick Sarmiento, who ran the Belvedere Hotel in Baltimore. This turned out to be a blessing.

I wish we could have done something to help the Gheens. When the news came that their twenty—three—year—old son, Kevin, a professional mountain climber, was killed in a fall in France. I stood at their outdoor memorial ceremony in upstate New York while my own son lay in a Baltimore hospital bed. I thought about whom I was mourning for. I was mourning for all of us. For the illnesses and accidents that touch us so randomly and without reason, for the loss of young people cut down in their prime.

Before we called Rick at the Belvedere Hotel, Enid made dozens of phone calls to rental agents and hotels, had maps of the area sent to us, and generally prepared us for the move to Baltimore. Rick Sarmiento sensed our desperation and became an immediate friend. He gave Enid and me a suite of rooms for $25 a night and a parking space for $10 a month. He gave Jackie a suite of rooms for $15 a night. He alerted the hotel personnel to our situation and tried in every way possible to give us back some of life's sweetness. I felt significant guilt about accepting his kindness. The grand old hotel was in the red, almost bankrupt really, still they were glad to have us. This situation made Rick's gesture seem all the more heroic.

Staying at a nice hotel in comfort may not seem like much, but it meant the world to us at the time. Two restaurants, a bar, and sundry small shops made up our new galaxy. Enid and I packed our clothing, took one small computer, and brought friendly pictures to replace the institutional ones hanging in the hotel rooms. We locked up the Peekskill home and didn't look back. We drove into Manhattan to pick up Evan and Jackie and packed their gear and computers into the car. The white station wagon looked like the old truck that was loaded for a trip to the West coast in the movie *The Grapes of Wrath*.

There was stuff tied on the roof rack. The back was full, and it was a tight fit even for two small people like Jackie and Evan. "This is ridiculous," said Evan. "It's too uncomfortable to travel like this, we're going to take the train." Enid and I drove the station wagon down to Baltimore by ourselves. We were worried about Evan going by train in his weakened condition, but Jackie was with him and it wouldn't have been helpful to argue. Evan and Jackie took an Amtrak train and arrived at the Belvedere Hotel at almost exactly the same time we did. We had just begun to unload the car when they came around the corner, off Charles Street.

It was a majestic hotel in its day. Very near the grandure and in the same milieu as the Plaza Hotel on fifth avenue in New York. It made our interludes between hospital stays bearable.

• • •

Years earlier, when Enid was still at Columbia and I was on the treadmill of work, we would plan meetings at the Plaza

Hotel for a weekend together, away from the kids and all the work around us that a thirty seven hundred square foot house and two and one half acres presented. Mrs. Bean, a rotund, smiling personality who stayed with the children, was a wonderful woman who could handle anything the kids could invent to frighten her away. They played the off-color records that had bolted many a housekeeper from our doorstep and she didn't even flinch.

When I planned a weekend with Enid it was PLANNED. We had a lot of catching up to do and a lot of straightening out of our lives as well. I wasn't happy to have her in school for so many of the children's early years. But I always remembered that she quit school when we first got married so I could pursue my career. I reserved a suite at the Plaza Hotel.

About three days before our rendevous, I usually dropped in at the Plaza to see what was booked for me. They had given me one of the new, small, rooms that looked out on the wall of an inner court. The young lady from the front desk took my consternation to heart and promptly showed me another suite that was superb and for the same amount of money. As she was showing me the suite she suddenly disappeared. Glancing into the boudoir I saw her lying on the bed, her hand patting the bed beside to her, inviting me for a quickie. Good God, don't people have complications enough. Doesn't she have anything better to do, I thought. "Let's go," I said brusquely and we took the elevator downstairs without another word between us. I signed for the room and ordered a dozen yellow roses to be sent up one hour before Enid's and my arrival.

Our rendevous date came with a cloudburst that lasted all day. I caught a cab to the hotel, registered and went up to the suite to dry out and wait for Enid. She was coming directly from class at Columbia and was driving in this mess. She would probably be a little late. Yes, the roses were there. The beautiful baroque chandelliers. The unimaginable old mouldings that connected every wall to every curved ceiling. The twelve foot square bathroom with a telephone. I was very aware of how privileged we had become.

Because Enid allowed me those years of struggle, and waited for her turn at school, our lives were changed. The children were not living in an atmosphere of ethnic hate, out of ignorance, as I had in Bangor. They grew up feeling and being told they were equal to everyone else. They grew up living in a home to be proud of. Parents to be proud of. We taught them right from wrong, the wonder and joys of extended family life but I did not teach them who they were as Jews, any better than my folks taught me. I taught them who they were as individuals and to be free but not about their ethnic roots.

"Hey kids, have you heard from mom?" I was calling home because Enid hadn't shown up yet and it was an hour past when I expected her. "Mom called us a long time ago and said she was leaving to meet you. Is something wrong dad," they said almost in unison. "OK I guess she's just caught in traffic," I said. Take care of each other and mind Mrs. Bean." Another hour and another call to the kids and still no Enid. We had been having some difficult quarrels about work, school and the kids and I was beginning to think she was standing me up. Enid's classes at Columbia brought her in touch with a different, faster living, group of mostly younger people. All her time was spent with these strangers. I was jealous and uneasy that I had no connection with or anything in common with them. I was angry that she wasn't with the children enough. Shit, would she really stand me up?

"Front desk," I querried. "This is Mr Handler. Have you perhaps seen my wife, is she in the lobby?" "Mr. Handler Your wife arrived about an hour ago and we sent her right up to your room," said the desk clerk. "You sent her up here? She's not here. Where did you send her," I asked? "We sent her up to your room," he said and proceeded to read me the number of the room that I had rejected three days ago.

After raising hell with him over the phone I went to the third floor suite to get her. I rang the bell and Enid answered the door, still dressed in her soggy clothes and still wearing her boots, because all the luggage was with me in our fifth floor suite. I was not in the mood for amenities. "Get your books and come with me," I ordered, practically dragging her to the elevator and up two floors to our room. She was about to return my abusive manner when, upon seeing this spacious suite and the dozen yellow roses, she realized what had happened. We both broke into laughter and fell into each others arms.

We were sitting in our underwear after we had stripped away our soggy clothes, and relaxing for a moment, when without a knock, the door burst open and a typical old New York bellhop barged in apologizing for the mixup in rooms and offering a bottle of Plaza scotch as a tonic for our wounded emotions. I blew my top, took the peace offering, threw him out. Then we laughed some more.

• • •

After the marrow graft had begun to resurrect his body, we brought Evan back to the Belvedere Hotel. As we pushed through the revolving front door trying to get past the lobby and

225

to the elevators to avoid any possible contact with germs that would attack his brand-new immune system, all of the bellhops, clerks, cleaning people, and residents whom Enid and I had lived with and wept to, stood and applauded this affirmation of life. I don't believe Evan understood what was happening at that moment, but no actor ever received more heartfelt and sincere applause than was given in that lobby.

Most of our days had been spent at the hospital, either in Evan's room, in the hallways, in the lunch room drinking coffee, or just talking in the large comfortable chairs of a lavish hospital lobby. It was in the lobby that I spent considerable time with some of Evan's actor friends who came to visit. Fisher Stevens and Rob Morrow were the two I remember the most.

They were poor struggling kids then. I was happy to pay for the coffee and lunches just to be with them. "You do weight lifting?" Rob said to me over cardboard coffee cups in a room set up just outside the cafeteria for families of patients who wanted solitude. That tickled me. Vanity wasn't dead yet. His comment gave me a glimpse into the time after all this would be over. The body, mind, and emotions were just waiting to return to a normal existence.

Their youthful antics (particularly Fisher's) and obvious good health helped give my mind a rest from the torture that Evan was going through upstairs. Rob and Fisher took Jackie out for several evenings of fun and drink to break the strain of her constant care giving. Jackie's mom, Sylvia, and I got to know each other for the first time sitting in that luxurious lobby.

Sylvia had come down from Connecticut to spend a little time with Jackie and, I felt, to discuss the length and depth of her commitment to Evan. I had been aware of Jackie's utter exhaustion for some time now, and as Sylvia and I spoke, the words just wouldn't stay down. "Why is Jackie still here?" I heard myself ask. "She loves him Murry, it's as simple as that." "Have you been discussing this with Jackie?" I asked, feeling this was the main reason for her visit. "Yes, and I don't know what to say to her anymore. Her youth is going by, her strength is waning, and every time I bring it up she starts to cry and says she can't leave because she loves him. I don't press it anymore."

What a bind she's in, I thought to myself. *I'm fighting for my son's life and she's fighting for her daughter's future.* We understood and sympathized with each other, and I came away with great respect for her directness and honesty. I was also astonished and in awe of Jackie's loyalty to Evan.

My blood wasn't good for Evan. How the hell can my blood not be good for my own son? It didn't seem fair to be pushed aside again, even if this time it was for chemical reasons. I felt worthless. Fortunately Enid's platelets were useful. And wonder of wonders, Bara, Enid's sister, had the magic potion. Her platelets were being accepted when his body rejected or just wouldn't make use of most others. When her arms were black and blue from being purged of platelets for Evan and she was obviously in pain, I was still jealous of her. Bara never faltered. She came and gave platelets every other day when she stayed in town, and she rushed down to Baltimore from New Jersey whenever the doctors said they needed her magic fluid.

Our nights at the Belvedere were reserved for sending letters, making telephone calls, washing Evan's pajamas and making frozen popsicles of different flavors to test their acceptance to Evan's taste buds. We tried peach, orange, cherry, and strawberry and finally wound up squeezing watermelons.

227

The watermelon was acceptable. He could taste it. Nothing really tasted good to him because his mouth and throat were raw and peeling from the chemotherapy drugs.

We sent out news and requests to our support network. When an emergency arose, we rushed back to the hospital. Many nights I ran back to sit with Evan because of the sudden pains that erupted in his liver or kidney areas. One night I found myself pushing his bed behind a young female orderly who was pulling on the front end. We were in the catacombs, the very bowels of the hospital, rushing toward the x-ray machine past bags of refuse and stored old equipment when his IV pole caught on a low cement beam on the ceiling. The woman up front didn't stop pulling and I envisioned the tubes pulling out and blood spurting from the hole in his chest as I pulled back in my direction, trying to offset her. It took a couple of loud yells from me to convince this gal that something was wrong. I think some hospital staff have become immune to others' pain. They see too much and just don't pay attention to it. She finally stopped pulling. I lowered the pole to get past the overhead obstacle, and we were on our way again. I glanced at Evan and I saw a look on his face that said, *he's really taking care of me.* What the hell did he think we were trying to do all these days that had suddenly turned into years. Shit, just let him live. These x-rays, as all the others they took of his organs, did not explain the severe pain or show any abnormalities.

I don't think Evan missed a single complication during his stay at Johns Hopkins. High fevers, fungus, and yeast attacks on the body with no means of protecting itself except with those same massive doses of antibiotics and that meant the violent, uncontrollable shake and bake. There were also blood

228

transfusions, dozens of them. We prayed, each time, that the hospital had cleansed the blood of all impurities.

• • •

Every other week I would try to get back to New York for a few days to look for some design and production work to help with the bills. My contacts were tapering off, and I began to rely more on those clients who had become real friends. Bill Canata at Pfizer, Elsa and Lorenzo Nadal at American Cyanamid International, and Joseph Feeks at PR Works were particularly kind. I'm not certain they knew the total desperation of my situation, but they must have sensed a great deal. I didn't spare anyone who would listen to my misery. It is impossible for me to explain how much these friends were responsible for my sanity.

Creating things was my way of life. Creating things of beauty was my inspiration. Besides running a business and raising children, I painted, wrote poetry, taught evening classes at The New School and The Fashion Institute, gardened, and designed Bonsai. Suddenly it was all taken from me. As Evan's basic life system was being taken from him, my vehicles for creativity, which were my life, were being taken away too.

My own self-worth had been badly damaged in the previous months by Evan's rejection of us and the medical community's rejection of my blood products to help him. These friends gave me back a feeling of worth and a sense of the continuing world outside, without which I might have faltered badly. There were other friends who had been closer to us over the years and were very disappointing in their reaction to our problems. Maybe I expected too much. I don't know what my response would have been had the tables been turned. I believe I would have done anything they asked of me. Knowing that you cannot count on friends in an emergency changes the friendship to a relationship on a different level.

Losing myself in work for a couple of days at a time was a blessing. I forgot, for a few moments, that leukemia was robbing me of my child, that our lives had been changed forever, no matter what the outcome. Then I would drive back to Baltimore, to my other real world.

15

Dad's Final Gift

Evan had been discharged from John Hopkins and was living, if you can call it that, in the old East Village apartment in New York City, The one I rented for the boys when they were students. Jackie was caring for him there.

Lowell and Evan were such happy, healthy kids when we first rented that apartment. It seemed like a lifetime ago. School, girlfriends, and dodging hookers on their way home in the evening were their only concerns. When they refused the hookers' invitations, the boys' manhood was questioned.

"You guys queers?" the girls would shout up the street.

"No, we have homework to finish for school tomorrow," they would respond. That story always cracked me up.

• • •

Enid and I did not see Evan on a regular basis. He was at the hospital at least once a week for tests when he wasn't resting at home. In this no—man's—land that he was in—getting his blood tested each week that said whether he would live or die, long hours of waiting to see the doctors, necessary blood transfusions, frightened of anyone who coughed or sneezed and with barely the strength to walk—he was not readily available to anyone but Jackie. This was the lowest valley in our relationship, a time of questioning motives and dreams, reality and illusion. I didn't know what was real anymore. I was tired of trying, praying, feeling guilty, and wondering what kind of son I would have if he lived.

It took two more years before Evan began to feel that he might survive. He kept looking over his shoulder (as we all did), waiting for a blood test to come back with the wrong numbers or a transfusion to carry HIV.

Very slowly, things started getting back to normal. I was looking for work again and beginning the process of reintroducing myself to the business world. Evan was into a similar but much more difficult process. Many of the people he met thought he had died. Producers did not want to take a chance on someone who might get sick in the middle of an expensive play or movie. It took time, confrontations with producers, and perseverance for Evan to break back into show business, but he did.

He tried coming home to Peekskill to recuperate with us when he was discharged, but the medical facilities were not responsive enough, nor did they take the care that was necessary for his immune-deficient condition. Enid desperately wanted to be able to care for him, but the poor medical care in Westchester County, one of the wealthiest in the entire country, would surely have killed him. It almost killed me.

• • •

Going to the local spa and exercising for an hour was old hat to me. I had been doing it for twenty—some years, long before it became popular. When we first moved to Furnace Dock

I would get the kids and Enid up an hour before school to do calisthenics. I stood on the round steps that led to the living room. Enid and the kids stood in the sunken living room in their pajamas, a fire roaring in the massive granite fireplace, and we did our thing. Hup, two, three, hup, two, three. Arms out, arms down, arms overhead. They hated exercising and hated me for forcing them. I knew that at six in the morning no sense of humor existed. Doing exercises didn't last long because Enid hated it most of all.

I went back to running on the treadmill at the spa at six in the morning, but something had changed. I used to run at four miles an hour, and I couldn't anymore. I could only sustain three and a half miles per hour. I guess those last five years with Evan's illness really beat me up. I discussed my lessening abilities with Enid, and she said, "You're just getting lazy. Go back and push." *She was right,* I thought, and threw myself into doing better.

The following week I could only do three miles an hour. What the hell was happening? The weather had turned colder and just walking from the car into the house had me panting as if I just ran a mile. Stairs became a difficult undertaking, and if nothing else our house was a series of staircases. A huge cement staircase in front leading to the massive, poured concrete deck. Stairs from my basement studio to the main floor and another to the upstairs. I was watching sick kids for so long it didn't dawn on me that I could get sick, too.

"What you're describing to me," said my brother—in—law, Arne Rosenheck, the oral surgeon, "sounds like a heart problem. Get to a doctor right away Murry. Today," he commanded. Now I may joke about Arne's shticks, but when it comes to diagnosing problems, I rank him with the best.

The next day I went to see the head of cardiology at the Peekskill Hospital. By this time, breathing was becoming a problem for me. I was given a fully wired stress test, during which I was injected with radioactive isotopes, then immediately put on a machine that circled me and took pictures of the material that was now pumping through my heart. In the middle of the process the power dipped then resumed. No one said a word, but I could see the expressions on their faces and the glances that went between the lab tech and the cardiologist. "We'll give you an appointment for the morning, Mr. Handler, and we will have the results. Everything looks okay so far," the doc said. Enid helped me get to the car, and she drove home. You know that I'm really sick when I let someone else drive.

That night was frightening. I felt like I was dying. I couldn't believe it, but I was. Arriving at the hospital the next day we were ushered into the doctor's office. "Have a seat Mr. Handler, the doctor will be right with you," the nurse said. From his office window, which overlooked the parking area, I saw the doctor get into his car and drive away.

"Nurse," I called, "wasn't that the doctor driving away?"

"No that couldn't be," lied the nurse, "he'll be with you in a moment."

Thirty minutes later I watched him drive back into the lot with a manila folder in his hand and run toward the office. "Mr. Handler," puffed the doctor coming through the door, "I'm sorry we didn't have the results waiting when you came in. The technician at the hospital is having difficulty reading the results because of the power dip yesterday. We could do another stress

234

test, but I believe you are fit as a fiddle. Nothing extraordinary showed up on your EKG. With your background of steady exercise, all you need to do is go back to the gym and work yourself into shape."

Not a picture to look at. I guess that envelope I saw in his hand as he ran toward the building was the non—results. As we closed the office door behind us, Enid and I looked at each other and knew we were in deep shit. I could barely breathe.

We got home and called Arne and related the two—day sequence of events, and I thought he was going to have his second heart attack. (He had his first when he was forty.) "Get down here immediately," Arne said, "I will call my group's cardiologist, he will know what it is."

When Arne's cardiologist got through with a long period of listening to my chest and moving me in different positions, he stood back and said, "Don't move fast" (as if I could) "don't do anything. You must have an angiogram. You're blocked somewhere. I think it's in the left anterior descending artery." This was a great medical team. They knew, with no hesitation, what the situation called for. They were only two hours from where I lived and in a less affluent area. Boy, was the Westchester medical community dumping on us.

"Look at the screen," said one of the doctors doing the angiogram procedure on me. The sudden flush of heat from the injected dyes was uncomfortable. "I don't know if we can get around that sharp angle when we do the angioplasty, but that blockage is 95 to 99 percent closed. It's lucky that the stenosis doesn't begin until after the first diagonal branch. I'm surprised you could walk in here." There it was, my once faithful heart, pumping away and deceiving me at the same time. "We don't have an opening to do the angioplasty right now, but we will try to schedule you in a week." *Uh oh, it's beginning to sound a bit like Peekskill*, I thought. At least I have some leverage here with Arne in this group. Maybe he can arrange it sooner.

I spent the next two nights in Enid's leather recliner in the library of our home, trying to stay alive and praying that no emergency would arise that would place me in the nearest hospital in Peekskill. I don't know who the hell I was praying to. Not Yahweh, the god of my people. Certainly not Jesus or Mohammed. Maybe I wasn't praying. Maybe it was a thought process that I have developed that feels like praying. Maybe it was to my inner self, the one place I could always count on for straight answers, the one place that put me in control.

The second night was a beaut. The nitroglycerin pills the doc gave me to put under my tongue whenever my chest felt like it was in a vise, stopped working. It was two in the morning, Enid was sleeping, and all I could think of was she's going to find me dead here in this fucking chair in the morning. The sun will come up and flood this room, and it will look beautiful, and I will be dead in this fucking chair in the morning.

One pill under the tongue, nothing. Two pills, nothing. Three pills, a tunnel all lit up and I was going down it. Someone must have pushed rewind because I was looking at people and places I hadn't seen in years and they were getting younger. A rather pleasant experience. *When I reach total rewind, will I be dead*, I wondered? I didn't want Enid to find me dead, damnit, but it didn't hurt at all, and there was music, too. The nitro kicked in hard, and I sat bolt upright, sucking air and wondering what world I was in.

The doctor's office called the next morning, and Enid drove me down to New Brunswick. I kept thinking that maybe they saw my vision of last night on their computer screen where they showed me my heart beating when they did the angiogram, and that's why they called me back earlier than expected.

The doctors cut me in both thighs, tubed me with a #5 French Introducer System—to you that's rubber tubes up the groin. Ballooned me, then put ten-pound sandbags on my incisions for eleven hours after the procedure. All the while I kept thinking, *Evan took this shit and a lot more. I can take it, too.*

When the nurses wheeled me into post op and I came out of my stupor, I saw that a small, red foil–wrapped chocolate heart had been placed on my chest as a treat. I came alive fast and blew my stack. "That's the kind of shit that put me here in the first place. Are you people crazy?" I shouted. From the looks on the nurses' faces, they thought *I* was the nut case. This wasn't fun and games anymore. I would have to protect myself as Evan had all those years in the hospitals.

The insurance company insisted that an overnight stay was not necessary. In other words, they wouldn't pay for it. Just as well. I had spent the day hassling with the head dietitian, asking for cooked vegetables, rice, and spinach, not the chicken hindquarters with fat and skin they brought to me.

"We're concerned about your protein, Mr. Handler. You must get enough protein," the dietitian said sweetly, as if talking to someone whose mind was gone. The only things gone from me was the heart blockage and my patience.

"Lady, I'm only going to be here for one day. The protein doesn't mean a thing for one day. Get this chicken off my tray and bring me what I asked for." She did.

Arne came to see me after my doctor had gone home. The doctor forgot to prescribe the painkiller that he said he would, and my lower back was in excruciating pain from the weight of those sandbags on my groins. Arne prescribed Tylenol with codeine, which worked wonders.

Late in that day, when I was discharged, Enid and Arne practically dragged me into the car and to the hotel down the street, where I collapsed for the night. Ninety—six dollars instead of the $500 the hospital would have charged. The insurance company wouldn't pay for a night's stay, and I couldn't have made the two—hour run home to Peekskill. Maybe the insurance companies will wise up someday. They could pay for a nearby hotel room and save about four hundred.

This was a frightening new world for me. Every ache, pain, or twitch anywhere near my chest and I was certain it was the end. I lost weight quickly. Nothing like fear to make you do something like pray, go to synagogue, believe. Fear is a great leveler. God is fear. I had prayed enough for Evan to cover me and all my progeny for all time to come. It's very funny when the realization hits you that you have been praying to fear all your life. Death, accident, and disease are completely arbitrary happenings, like a snowflake landing on your shoulder.

"You have heart disease," the Westchester doctor monitoring me after recovery kept telling me.

Each time I would answer, "I had an angioplasty, I'm okay now."

"You have heart disease, Mr. Handler," he would counter. He made his point.

I drove Enid absolutely crazy. "No fat, no seeds on the bread, they have fat in them. Only skim milk. I will eat absolutely nothing that used to be alive," I would shout. I was impossible. I hated eating this way, hated the whole damn situation.

When I gave my medical history to Arne's heart man down in New Brunswick, he stopped me when I told him, "My dad had his first angina attack at fifty."

"You're in better shape than your dad. That's why you didn't get caught until you were sixty-two," said the doc. "It's in the genes, Murry. Sooner or later you were going to get it. If you must have something wrong with your heart this is about the best thing. It took sixty years of bad eating and slowly came on you. It didn't kill you. It warned you in time. You're one of the lucky ones."

I hadn't looked at it that way. Why couldn't dad have given me his big nose instead? He had a shnoz like Jimmy Durante. It would have been more obvious but a lot safer. I could have had a nose job.

• • •

The kids were living on their own now. We were empty nesters. It was great, but since my angioplasty the house was too much for me to handle. I was afraid to take down trees anymore or split wood. Raking an acre of front lawn really wasn't what I wanted to do with the rest of my life, a life that I suddenly realized was fragile and limited in time. The snowy winters I used to love became my nemesis. Until this happened, I honestly didn't realize I was getting older. I guess I should be thankful for that.

Our homestead, with twenty-six years of life and sweat equity in it, had to go. This was difficult for us. How would the kids take it? Where would they come home to? We very much identified with this house and land. Lowell and I built the shed together. Enid and I worked endless hours fixing and painting and living through our five-year projects. Lil and Evan never really knew any other home. Suzie, our mongrel dog who only liked women, was buried out back under the big oak, beyond the flat white rock.

We had two dogs, Suzie, the mongrel whom I put down when she was twelve, and a black Labrador retriever named Soul. We got the Lab when Suzie was eight, and Suzie bossed her around for about two years, then Soul turned the tables. They lived out back in a bottom—heated double dog house I designed and built. Each dog had her own door, and in the winter the small inner space had a common wall so the warmth of their bodies pressed against the same partition.

When Susie got old and started wandering around in a lost state, I would go out in a winter storm and find her half buried in the snow. The family held a conference and decided she was suffering too much and had to be put down. The last time, it was three weeks before we found her, and she was afraid of us. She didn't know who we were.

This was the girls dog, Enid's and Lil's. Suzie didn't like men. When the morning came to bring her to the vet, Lil and Enid got in their cars and ran away. I was left standing in the driveway, cursing both of them under my breath. The dirty job of taking Suzie to be put down was mine. "It would be easier for you," they said. "You aren't as attached as we are."

I held Suzie gently on that cold stainless—steel tabletop in the vet's office. "Put your hand over her mouth in case she nips at us, Mr. Handler," the vet said. Then he injected her. She let out a small groan, more like a sigh of relief, and went limp in my arms. I didn't expect the wave of feeling that came over me. I started to cry. I just stood there and cried, didn't make any noise, just a wet, silent cry for a dog that wasn't mine and a life that slipped away in my arms.

The doctor, seeing how distressed I was, quickly bundled Suzie into a black plastic bag and led me to my car via a special side entrance. I wasn't going to let a stranger bury her. The doc had asked me if he should dispose of her. I couldn't let him. "No, not in the seat next to me doc, in back please," I said. I didn't want that still—warm body next to me. I couldn't stand it.

I drove Suzie home, cursing the women I loved, lifted the plastic bag out of the back seat, and held it away from me so her body wouldn't bump against mine. I took the slate walk around the front of the house, ducked under the low limb of the Japanese maple on the back lawn, walked past the white rock we used to run around for exercise, and dug a hole beneath the giant oak on the edge of the front acre just where the deep woods began. I buried Susie plastic bag and all. I covered the grave with large slabs of field rock and stood a few paces back. I guess she was my dog after all.

Soul was primarily Lil's dog. We bought her for Lil's sixteenth birthday. "We can't keep her anymore, Lil," I said over the phone. "Will you take her?" Lil who lived in Lancaster, Pennsylvania at this time, was married to Tom and they had a dog of their own. When we gave Soul to Lil and Tom we didn't know that Soul was sick. When Soul died three months later, we were as surprised as they were. That was the last of our animals. No more horses, dogs, cats, snakes, or gerbils. It was time to concentrate on ourselves.

With the dogs gone and Evan surviving four years after his transplant, Lowell married and living in Cold Spring, and Lil having babies in Lancaster, we put the house on the market and accepted an offer to close in three months. At this same time, John and Rosemary Morace, those wonderful people from the wine group who made their apartment in New York available to us when Evan was in Memorial Hospital, decided to have a wine tasting at their villa in Tuscany, Italy. All of the wine tasting bunch was invited. Enid and I accepted and then rented a villa of our own through an ad in the *New York Times*, for the three weeks to follow the five day stay at John and Rosemary's. The rented house was in the foothills of the Apennine Mountains. We looked forward to a month of fun and rest to regain emotional and physical strength and prepare for the move to our next life in the Triangle area of North Carolina.

It was the second time Enid and I had visited the Morace villa in Tuscany. The first time was on a vacation before Evan got sick. This was like stepping back into the pages of time. Their spread was about fifteen acres of vineyards and olive trees in the rolling hills of Tuscany. Enid and I stayed on the second floor of the guest house, about 1,000 feet from the main house on the other side of the vines and olive trees.

Five years ago there had been no olive trees only grapes, and it was harvest season then. We arose each morning at 5 a.m. and went to the vines for picking. This wasn't required, just something we wanted to do to get the feel of the land and show our gratitude to our hosts. The men of the village who had hired on to harvest that years crop, scoffed at Enid and me for wanting to help but four days later when we inadvertently slept in they complained to John, now addressed as Padron, that they were counting on our picking. When the leader of the village pickers first handed out the grape cutters, he handed me a plain pair of shears. That's all that was left. Although the scissors cut into my hand and it became very uncomfortable, I made certain that I picked faster than the villager facing me on the other side of the row and even reached over and swiped a bunch or two from his side as I went. He didn't like it, but as far as I was concerned they had turned this into a macho matter and I was ready and willing. This kind of fight was a relief, and a lot of fun compared to the fights Enid and I had been in recently.

Enid picked as well as anyone, and all the pickers from the town of Cole Val D'Elsa began to take notice of us. Next to drinking the wine, eating lunch with the Padron in the head man's house was the best. Braised rabbit in red sauce, pasta, fresh salad, and plenty of local Chianti. What could be better? A challenge in the morning, a great earthy lunch, then off to explore Tuscany.

From the balcony of our second—floor guest house suite, we could see the towers of San Giminano. Between us and San Giminano, six miles away, was nothing but softly rolling hills dotted with sheep, a field here and there of golden wheat, and an occasional clump of trees. The shades of earth tones was indescribable against a light blue sky. And the quiet! No wonder the Renaissance started here.

Was all this beauty here while Evan had been suffering the unimaginable? How can God hold beauty and pain side by side and ignore the suffering? Is there a balance of good and evil that must be kept?

The four days at John and Rosemary's tasting were wonderful, and although my diet and my fear kept me from eating much of anything that used to be alive, it didn't inhibit my wine drinking. Pasta and wine are not the worst things to be relegated to, and John's wines were getting better.

I was glad when we left for our rented villa. I wanted to rest and dream without people around me, without making communal decisions. I was tired of making decisions for anyone but myself. I wanted to learn how to be selfish and carefree. I yearned to be young again, free of memories and disease.

We drove west to the coast just above Livorno. We took the coastal route north, skirting Viareggio, and then west away from the beach, just below Pietrasanta, into the mountains toward Pedona. All the people we asked for directions just laughed and moved their finger in a spiraling, upward motion in the air. Finally someone who spoke a combination of halting English and hand signs showed us where the road to Pedona was. If you didn't live there, you would never know there was a village in the clouds. Now we understood the spiraling finger and the laughter. It was a tiny road that went at forty five degree angles up the mountain, like a fire escape with tiny landings. Every time we came to a turn Enid covered her eyes and I leaned on the horn to let the car coming down from the other side know that I was there. It was terrifying. Only one car could go around a turn at a time, and all at the same sharp angle. If we weren't so terrified we might have enjoyed the spectacular views that presented themselves at intervals between the trees. I swore, all the way up, that if I made it to the top I'd never come down again.

The village was built on two levels, the remains of a medieval castle or fort, and the narrow, attached homes with common outside walls snaked along the ridge like the Great Wall of China. There wasn't much of a town. Two restaurants (not open at your convenience) a general store and a grocer. Most of the upper level was the homes of people who worked below and could afford the clean air and spectacular views. In the letter we received from the ad in the *Times* we were directed to get the key from a certain family who ran one of the restaurants. At the restaurant we were told that the man was in the fields, key in pocket. We sent his son for him to get the keys and for some reason he disappeared, too. We lost our patience and began to get testy. I would not bribe them to get what I already had paid for. The key finally appeared.

Our rented house was really nice. From every window, nothing but mountains as far as the eye could see. Past the mountains, about ten miles east, the ocean at Viareggio was visible on most days. When the sun rose and set here, you didn't watch it, you were part of it. The fenced—in back yard had two large fig trees, and the fruit was ripe and dripping. It was gluttony at first sight. The kitchen was well outfitted, and the rooms were comfortable.

Each morning, across a strangely configured crossroad, I walked to the general store for fresh bread. The loaves were too large for us, so the lady proprietor cut off whatever sized chunk we wanted and weighed it. Life became simple, except for getting up and down the mountain.

I painted two watercolors of the mountains from the back of the local tavern. The lady who owned the tavern gave me a pail with water and a comfortable chair and table to work at on the deck that hung off the mountain just outside her tavern. I had the paintings framed when I got home and kept a promise to my cousin Gerry, who had asked me before I left to do a sketch for him. My drawings and paintings are like my babies, I just don't give them away. But this was different. Gerry was Gail's husband, Gail, my little cousin in the tutu. Gail from so long ago in the Handelsman/Haines house in Forest Hills. Gerry had fallen on hard times physically. He was confined to a wheelchair in a small second—floor, no elevator apartment, on Long Island. He is one of the sweetest guys I ever met, and he gets struck down. No reason, no explanation. Gerry is right up there next to Evan and Lowell when it comes to being brave. It made me so happy when he called to thank me for the sketch. If I were a god, I wouldn't have let this happen to him.

16

Leaving Somanydoors

The huge, rusting dumpster in the driveway was almost full. When the moving company brought it I thought they were crazy. "We don't have enough stuff to throw out that will even cover the bottom of that thing," I said.

"We'll see," said the man from the moving company.

Enid and I had just returned from our trip to Italy and the race was on to pack and get all our closing papers for them in order. I began to think that squeezing in a month in Tuscany then running home to pack wasn't such a good idea. This was on Enid's schedule not mine. I didn't like rushing from one thing to another. We had thirty—six hundred square feet of home to empty and twenty—seven years of hoarding to discard.

The kids couldn't take much. Their homes were too small. We gave Grandma Fran's dining room set to Lil. Lowell got our big, old, black leather chair; Evan, because he lived in an apartment, could only take a few small pieces. He took a lead glass ice cream bowl with an overall diamond cut, and the star of David cut deeply into the bottom, that came from Enid's grandmother; a miniature display cabinet; and a large, primitive, green pie safe. He thought it was just an old cupboard until a New York antiques dealer offered him $600 worth of anything in his shop in exchange. We tried to keep all we could in the family. We still treasured furniture that we inherited from Fran's house after she had died. They were all full of memories.

Enid and I found memorabilia we had long forgotten and suddenly couldn't live without. As the weeks of packing continued, we found ourselves less and less attached to things that were really meaningful and in our exhaustion we tossed items out we probably should have kept. Again and again I found myself staring blankly at an object I hadn't seen in years, enveloped by the sudden stream of memory that poured from it; a book, a bust of Enid in ceramic unfired clay I made when she was fifteen, business cards from former clients and friends that brought back faces and places, love letters my father—in—law sent to Fran, wedding invitations in Hebrew and English from three generations past, my mother's plastic bracelets that I could almost hear clacking when they hit together as she moved her arms. And the pictures, especially the pictures.

"Mrs. Handler," the wife of the moving van driver called up to us from the dumpster in the driveway, "Mrs. Handler are you sure you want to throw this out? You must have made a mistake," she said, waiving a large photo album in her hand. The driver and his wife dropped by periodically to go through the house to judge how many boxes we were packing and how many trips the small truck would have to make down the road to where the big van would be loaded. Our driveway was too narrow for a van that size. With three—foot granite walls on both sides of an eight—foot—wide curved driveway, there was no way the moving van could negotiate it. The van that would actually take our stuff to North Carolina was in a parking lot down the road in front of a small diner.

The driver's wife was right, we *had* made a mistake. This throwing out of old things, was a peculiar habit that has continued with Enid for all our lives together. If it wasn't being used or was not the style she wanted at this time, she would trade up or throw it out if I wasn't there to stop her.

The driver's wife was holding an old picture and memento album with solid wood covers and Enid's name in script cut out of wood nailed to the cover. The rain the night before hadn't done too much damage because the weight on top of the album and the solid wood cover kept the inside pages tightly closed and dry. It was a high school memento album that started in 1947, and the last picture in it shows the party at the Barricinni Candy Factory, given for Enid in celebration of her engagement to me. All of Enid's early boy and girlfriends up to that time were pictured and named. Thank you, driver's wife, wherever you are now. We were getting tired and careless in our decisions to get rid of stuff. We tried to concentrate harder.

We had two weeks left to get out. I literally kept my head in a carton since our return from Italy. Enid was on the phone constantly with our attorney and the town of Croton's tax office. The town inspector wouldn't issue us a certificate of occupancy, which was necessary to complete the sale of Somanydoors, because the last step going down to what had become my studio from the main floor was one inch shorter than the rest of the steps.

In our second five-year fix-up plan, when we combined the garage and basement into one large space to make the downstairs into a TV room, we had a new cement floor poured.

That accounted for the step difference but, at the time, I never thought it was an issue. The Brennan brothers, our builders at the time, were the best I had ever used but they didn't advise me of any codes.

"Was there a bathroom in the basement when you purchased the house, or did you put it in?" the inspector asked.

We told him, "That's the way it was when we bought it."

He then demanded affidavits that the house had been built before the building codes became law. He wasn't nice about it either. It was more like an order with a threat. He knew the house had been built in 1935. He knew it was not recorded at his office because it predated the town's records.

No one that we knew of was alive to make the needed verification. I felt certain that what he really wanted was a payoff, but I wouldn't offer him anything. I was too angry to offer anything. I had been in this place before with stronger personalities than his. We paid taxes on this place for twenty seven years and the town didn't say don't pay taxes because the last step is too short. This could screw up our entire sale of the house, and I had already rented a house in North Carolina. What a mess.

We weren't getting anywhere with the townies. Enid sat in their offices for hours and argued that no one was alive or accessible or known to us who could verify what they were asking about. The smug bastards wouldn't budge. They seemed certain that we would have to kick in, meanwhile we continued packing.

"You can't close a deal on a house without a certificate of occupancy," our attorney kept telling us. We knew that, but we had to keep packing and hope for the best. If the worst happened, maybe the buyer would give us more time to get the certificate. More than likely he would try to renegotiate the price. "Never give a sucker a chance" seemed to be the good advice of the day. Maybe the inspector would fall and break his neck on that last step.

Unknown to us, Lowell's wife, Susanna, had been working on a project with the Croton town attorney. She made one of her weekly stops to talk with Enid and we told her what was happening to us. "Let me make a few calls She said, there may be something I can do." We never found out just what she did, but on the last day, as the moving men were taking out the furniture, we instructed them not to the fax machine, our only contact for signatures with our New York City attorney. Enid got a phone call to come down to the Croton City Hall. They signed off on our certificate, all the while berating Enid. There was nothing gracious about their capitulation. Enid came home from Croton, and we plugged the fax back in for another minute, sent the signed certificate to our attorney, then allowed the movers to take it all.

• • •

A few weeks before our move I had driven down to Chapel Hill, North Carolina, and raced around for two days with Enid's cousin Barbara Cohen looking for a nice house to rent that was near shopping and could hold all our cartons until we built on our land.

A couple of years earlier, real estate developer Kevin Huggins and I had become friends through the many months Enid and I were looking for land. He sold us seven acres, just eight miles south of Chapel Hill, at Indian Landing in Chatham County. When Barbara heard that Enid and I had purchased land in North Carolina, she immediately purchased a parcel in the same place and moved with her husband, Sheldon, to a house they had rented to wait for us.

The rented house in Chapel Hill would be our base of operations until we built on the seven acres. The seven acres was in two contiguous parcels of three and four acres and comprised a small island of land between the entrance to the Indian Landing development and an old stagecoach road that ran from Chatham County to Durham, North Carolina. We had access to the land from both roads. Up Stagecoach Road on a bluff in back of our property was what was left of the large farm that had previously owned all this land. They still had sheep and other critters, and it gave me a comforting feeling knowing that we were still connected to the past.

Our acreage was on a bluff of hardwoods and holly, some so big I couldn't get my arms around them. Wonderful granite outcroppings with green moss patterns splaying across the boulders reminded me of our Hudson River house. I couldn't wait to build.

• • •

We waived goodbye to the driver and his wife. "See you in Chapel Hill in four days," we shouted as they left the driveway with the last of the small truck loads. It was Friday and they would park their monster moving van over the weekend, then start out for North Carolina on Monday.

We had two cars to take down there, and Enid made me really proud of her. We loaded her car, a 1987 Acura, with thirteen cases of wine; 1978 Bordeaux made up about eight of these cases. The rest was an amalgam from the world's wine-growing areas. Ten years earlier I had developed an interest in wine and I read about and tasted nearly everything that came on the market. Dinner guests listened in silence - I suddenly knew what I was talking about. Sommeliers stopped butting in when I ordered, and the fear that most of us have when presented with a daunting wine list vanished. It was pure power.

A local wine merchant, Pat Cippalone, needed a logo and stationery designed, and we decided to swap services. The bill came to about $2,000, and I recall Pat eagerly beginning to pile bottles of Chianti and Asti Spumante into my basket as his payment to me.

While designing his job I began to read about wine, and in the two months until his logo was acceptable to him I had become something of a wine maven. I stopped him and said, "No, Pat, I will choose them myself," and proceeded to take his entire stock of 1961, 1966, and 1970 Bordeaux.

Pat was taken aback and said, "Murry, you took all of my great 61s."

"Yes, Pat," I answered, "but you taught me that as a merchant it's all for sale and it can only be sold once." That's how my wine cellar started.

Wine collecting was becoming almost an obsession. Our basement had two—feet—thick stone walls and maintained a naturally cool and consistent temperature. I closed off a six—by—ten-foot area that jutted out under the massive cement and stone staircase that led to the front door. It was perfect for storing wine. As the years rolled by I lost track of the bottle count and the unopened cases lying on the floor shoved under the bottom shelves. But I knew pretty much where everything was and what was there. I did label one wall of bottles that were the better French Bordeaux and I continued to buy most of my wine from Pat.

When Enid and I entertained it was so much fun and such a privilege to go downstairs to the wine cellar and choose from almost any wine region in the world. I learned history and geography for the first time in my life, from the wine region maps that hung all around the walls, because it related to something that interested me. Now those treasured bottles were heading South in Enid's car.

. . .

The car I drove south, a white 1983 Olds wagon, was loaded with bonsai trees. Wine and bonsai were two rich man's hobbies for the Bangor kid. I felt very comfortable with them. Twenty—seven years earlier Enid had showed an interest in bonsai, and I purchased a book and a set of tools for her. She never used any of it. I don't even remember her reading the book. I made the mistake of reading it. It would become, for me, a lifetime of studying this living art form.

Enid followed me in her car all the way down and drove like a trooper. It wasn't an easy one—day drive, and following someone makes it more difficult. We couldn't stop at a motel with what we were transporting. We planned to stop at Barbara and Sheldon's house. By this time Sheldon had a position teaching shop at the Roanoke Rapids high school, just south of the Virginia border and three hours from our Chapel Hill destination. We stayed overnight with them, lightened our wine bottle load by two, and continued the next morning into Chapel Hill. Enid hadn't seen the house I rented and happily, she was delighted with the choice. It was in a small cul de sac about three minutes from great shopping and five minutes from the center of town. The cement driveway was only one car width, but long enough for two end to end and was protected from the neighbors by a ten-foot tall hedge shrub we came to know as Red Tips. All the wine cases went into the coldest room in the house. Basements down here were scarce because the soil was clay and wet. I put my bonsai out on the back deck and in the large screened porch. The house had four bedrooms, three of which we used to store our unpacked cartons until we could find a builder for our land at Indian Landing. It was beginning to feel like home.

The movers arrived in Chapel Hill on Tuesday, and we settled into the very comfortable house. While we settled in and tried to find things in cartons, we also began to search for a contractor to build our dream home.

During the years at Somanydoors, Enid and I had become successes in our chosen professions and in life. My Dad, Grandma and Grandpa, Aunt Alfreda, Uncle Lou, Aunt Bella and aunt Esta had died. Both of Enid's parents died. Lowell was diagnosed with Tourette syndrome and was coping with it. Evan got leukemia and beat it. Lil got married and delivered us grandkids, and I developed heart disease. The defining part of our lives as a family unit living together on Furnace Dock Road was over. It was time for a new beginning.

CONCLUSION

I hadn't intended writing a book, a real book that is. I was already past seventy, the years were going by at such a fast pace and my kids were having kids who might not remember me. I wasn't sure my own children really knew who I was, where I came from or what they meant to me. We had been through brimstone and hell together with Lowell's Tourette Syndrome and Evan's leukemia. I wanted to leave something tangible, something they could go back to if they needed clarification or even just a story to believe in and tell to *their* grandkids.

So, one day I said to Enid, "I'm going upstairs to write my memoir". Enid, without looking up said, "OK". After all, the boys both had their memoirs published.

Nine months later I came downstairs with a manuscript. Nine years later I think it's ready to print. I wasn't working on it constantly. Much of my time was consumed by my painting, shows of my work and just living.

256

But '*Almost* A Jew' was never far from my mind. It began to define me and gave me understanding of my early years that I hadn't been able to reach before. I began to understand why I acted or reacted, as I did, to different situations. To my surprise I found that the boy, Murry, was a super sensitive kid filled with fear and apprehension. I simply had no one to follow, no one to teach me, talk to me, walk with me—until Enid put her arm in mine. I had my first real friend and my first introduction to a world that looked beyond nail—hanging survival.

The Catholic Church played a role in my youth that left me with guilt about killing their God. As a child, I had no idea what Catholics were talking about. As I read and understood, as the church changed its message, they freed not only their own but me, a Jew, as well. They pardoned me for an unpardonable crime that I never committed.

My view now is that Nature is our Mother and our God. We, collectively, are committing the unpardonable crime by killing Nature on our planet. Destruction of our planet is the true death of God.

For why is all around us here as if some lesser god had made the world, but had not force to shape it as he would.

"Idylls of the King" *Tennyson*

www.ingramcontent.com/pod-product-compliance
Lightning Source LLC
Chambersburg PA
CBHW030415100426
42812CB00028B/2964/J